CAT ON THE CAY

The Honorable Harriet S. Wymbs
Illustrations by Fran Swarbrick

SKYLINE Publications, Inc.
Boca Raton, FL

Cat on the Cay

CONTENTS

Chapter I *1*

Chapter II *5*

Chapter III *11*

Chapter IV *15*

Chapter V *17*

Chapter VI *25*

Chapter VII *29*

Chapter VIII *37*

Chapter IX *41*

Chapter X *43*

Chapter XI *47*

Chapter XII *53*

Chapter XIII *59*

Chapter XIV *63*

CAT ON THE CAY

Copyright © The Honorable Harriet S. Wymbs 1997
All Rights Reserved

No part of this book may be reproduced, in any form, by photocopying or by any electronic or mechanical means, including information storage or retrieval systems, without permission in writing from both the copyright owner and the publisher of this book.

LCCC 96-071167
ISBN 1-889936-04-9

SKYLINE Publications, Inc.
Boca Raton, FL

Printed in the Canada

First Edition - September 1997
2 3 4 5 6 7 8 9 10

The sale of this book without its cover is unauthorized. If you purchased this book without a cover, you should be aware that it was reported to the publisher as "unsold and destroyed." Neither the author nor the publisher has received payment for the sale of this "stripped book."

Chapter XV	65
Chapter XVI	71
Chapter XVII	75
Chapter XVIII	85
Chapter XIX	89
Chapter XX	93
Chapter XXI	101
Chapter XXII	111
Chapter XXIII	117
Chapter XXIV	121
Chapter XXV	131
Chapter XXVI	135
Chapter XXVII	141
Chapter XXVIII	145
Epilogue	159

* * * *

INTRODUCTION

Cay Cay, Bahamas

Cat Cay (pronounced "Key") is a small island, two and one quarter miles long, and a half mile at the widest. Located on the western edge of the Great Bahama Bank and just south of Bimini, this small bit of paradise is only a half-hour flight from Miami and about one hour from Palm Beach. This tiny isle is made up of limestone, coral and sand. Palms, Pines and other tropical trees grow in abundance as well as a profusion of multicolored flowering shrubs and plants. Once the hideout of notorious pirates, Morgan and Blackbeard, it is now residence to a few lucky homeowners. One of the world's outstanding playgrounds, the island also hosts a private resort, the Cat Cay Club.

* *

The Bahamas were discovered on October 12, 1492 by Christopher Columbus, who landed on the island of San Salvador. He was greeted by friendly Arawaks — they called themselves, "Ceboynas". Columbus, however, called them Indians, as he was confident he had landed on the coast of Oriental India.

Through history, the Bahamas have been under the flags of both Spain and England. Under the Treaty of Versailles, they became a part of the British Empire.

The original deed to Cay Cay was granted to Captain William Henry Stuart, in 1874 by Queen Victoria, as compensation for his services as "Keeper of the Lighthouses".

Captain Haigh, the scion of a wealthy and titled English family, later held title to this little island. The Island custom of dressing for dinner each evening, in accord with British colonial tradition, which is still widely practiced, can be attributed to this fine English gentleman.

After the American Revolution, thousands of Loyalists left the colonies for lands still under the Union Jack. Many fled to the Bahamas where they were granted "unoccupied lands" by the King of England. Today, their descendants are well represented throughout the native population on most islands of the West Indies.

During the U.S. Civil War, Cat Cay served as a base for Confederate blockade runners. During World War II, the Allied Forces used Cat Cay as a secret crash base for PT boats, damaged in their Atlantic patrols.

**

The intriguing name "Cat Cay" could have come from several popular West Indian legends. The island does have an extensive cat population, of the domestic variety. It is well known that felines were used aboard sailing ships, to control the rodent population. The original cats were most probably cast ashore from these ships, some of which had foundered on nearby reefs. Another plausible story is that the islands' shape resembles the "Cat Head", a prominent piece of architecture on the bows of old sailing ships.

**

Chapter 1

    The early years of my life were rootless and lonely. I was an only child of ambitious parents who's future was always molded by corporate promotions. Advancement meant more to my father than putting down roots in one home or even in one community. The genes I inherited from my agricultural ancestors were truly frustrated by our constant moves across the United States. I wanted permanent friends, a pet, and a yard where I could watch things grow from season to season and year to year.

    I was five years old when we settled in the small town of Newton, Iowa. It was a trading center for the huge farming community surrounding it and the corporate headquarters for the Maytag Corporation. My father was joining the financial division of this rapidly developing company and his future appeared to be promising.

My school career started in Mrs. Cleo Starr's kindergarten. I could hardly believe my good fortune to have been thrust into a world of fun and games with 20 other jolly children and a teacher who enjoyed the activities as much as we did. She noticed my shyness and drew out of me the fear I had of throwing myself into a relationship that might be withdrawn by yet another move to another city. After all, Newton was my fifth home in five years. She took a very special interest in me and my parents and she became a very stabilizing influence in my life.

It was Mrs. Starr who encouraged my friendship with a moon faced little girl named Betty Ladd. Betty lived the life I dreamed about. Her father owned a large farm five miles outside the town limits. Betty's brothers were so much older than she, that in many ways she, too, was treated like an only child. One of her three huge brothers drove her to school each morning in the family truck, while the rest of us got there by walking. I was usually waiting in the school yard when she arrived in the battered old farm vehicle.

It wasn't long before I had wormed an invitation to come for a weekend visit to the Ladd farm. It took some real work on my part to convince my father it was more important for him to drive me to the Ladd farm on Saturday morning than it was for him to play his usual golf game at the Country Club. I still vividly remember that 1924 trip in our model 'T' Ford. It was a crisp early fall morning and the Iowa clay road was firm under the car wheels. I had never been away from home over night except at my grandparents, but I had no

Chapter 1

qualms about leaving my father and rushing into the arms of Betty's parents.

I was led into a very large, very old white frame house that was filled with the odors of Saturday morning baking. Betty and I each received a fresh piece of cake to take with us into the large back yard. As Betty showed me the windmill and the pump that provided their drinking water, two big collies lumbered up to us and nudged their noses against our bare legs. I was terrified because I had never before been in contact with big dogs. Betty's brothers were forced to come and get the dogs before I would stop crying.

To change the mood, Betty raced off through the corn fields with me following. We ended up in the barn where we climbed up to the loft and jumped into the piles of straw below. When we were exhausted from this activity we took baskets and filled them with fresh eggs from the chicken coop. We picked dried ears of corn from the fields and fed the active squealing pigs. By now I was beginning to feel more at home around the farm animals.

Betty asked me if I liked cats, and I didn't know what to say. I had never played with one. She led me to an old storage shed. There on a pile of rags a mother cat was sheltering her litter of kittens. After much oohing and aahing, we each selected a squirming kitten and carried them back to the house. We spent some happy hours on the kitchen floor feeding and playing with our charges. I was enchanted beyond words with these squiggly little creatures who nipped us with their sharp teeth one minute and snuggled and purred against us a minute later. I hated it when we were told to return them to their mother. I decided then and there that someday I would have a cat of my very own so I would never have to give it up.

We lived in Newton for 3 years before the Maytag Corporation transferred my father to the Chicago area. Those years were filled with frequent visits to the Ladd farm and ending my friendship with Betty was a very sad moment in my life.

Chapter 2

By the time I was ten years old I was entering my sixth school and living in my eighth town. Betty Ladd still remained the only true friend I had ever known and my dream of having a pet cat was still just a dream. Gold fish were the only pets I had nurtured and they were usually flushed down the toilet when we made a hasty move.

My father had risen to the position of Treasurer of the Maytag Finance Corporation, a subsidiary of the appliance manufacturer, headquartered in Chicago. We moved into a luxury apartment in fashionable mid-town Evanston, Illinois. My parents had a handsome new Nash automobile and I was sporting an expensive two wheel sidewalk bike around my new neighborhood. I heard my father boast that he was a paper millionaire, which meant that the margined stock he held in Maytag Corporation was worth approximately one million dollars. We were truly on top of the world, that is, until the bubble burst in the stock market crash of 1929.

Overnight, people like my father had lost their paper fortunes. Companies like Maytag Finance Corp. were closing their doors. With no one buying new appliances, financing was no longer needed.

Mother had forced my father to put a certain amount of his monthly earnings into a savings account. It was that money that kept us alive until my father landed a new job in 1932. Although he had stayed with Maytag until the company books were closed, in 1930 we had to leave our lovely apartment and settle for less expensive quarters in the south end of town. This was a crowded area where buildings often had less than five feet separating them from each other. We were fortunate to have moved into a building that looked down upon a row of old wood frame houses that had not been replaced by new development before the crash. Once again I found myself adjusting to a whole new world.

There were only two other girls in our apartment building. The janitor's daughter, Elaine, was nine years old and lived with her parents in the basement apartment. Above us, on the third floor lived a Swiss emigrant couple and their seven year old daughter Peggy. They had strong German accents and strange customs, the odors of cooking food coming from their kitchen were entirely alien to my sense of smell.

The old house next to our building was rented by a large family. I could watch their activities from my bedroom window, the children, ranging from teen-agers down to babies were a grubby, noisy lot. The whole family seemed to be constantly

Chapter 2

fighting and screaming at each other. The house had no screens over the windows and the children climbed in and out like monkeys tumbling out of their cages. They would drop to the porch roof and jump to the ground from there. I didn't think I had much chance of surviving a friendship with the Roberts' kids next door, so I introduced myself to Elaine and she accepted my friendly overture. Elaine already played with Peggy, so we became a threesome, even though I was much older at eleven years of age.

    Elaine's mother hired out as a cleaning lady to families in the huge water front homes along Lake Michigan's shores. Her father was always busy with maintenance work around the apartment building, and Elaine had household duties to take care of when she returned from school. Her mother would leave notes telling her the special things she should do, besides setting the table for dinner. She was not supposed to invite other children into the apartment when her parents were not there. Her two older brothers were also supposed to stay outside after school, however, when they knew their father would be tied up for a long time on a difficult repair job, they would invite their friends to come in and play. The boys would head for their own room and Elaine, Peg and I would occupy the living room, all the while keeping our ears tuned for the possible return of Mr. Petersen. When we stayed outside, our only playground was the ugly cement slab behind our apartment building. Rows and rows of wet laundry were usually waving in the wind, and if we soiled anything as we dodged between rows we were in big trouble with our elders.

From this ground level, the only way we could spy on the Roberts' kids was through the cracks in the dilapidated, unpainted six foot wood fence that separated our yard from theirs. We were forbidden to associate with them, but this didn't mean we couldn't spy on them. Many days, after school our main activity was peering through fence cracks and discussing what we observed on the other side. The Roberts' were great for playing ball games in which the family dogs challenged the children for control of the ball. They were wild, raucous, and sometimes dangerous affairs. The family cats often ended up being tossed into the fray, screaming and snarling at the indignity. Mrs. Roberts either was not at home when the children got out of school, or she was deaf, because she never interfered in the children's play.

We were never able to figure out how many cats lived with the Roberts' clan. It was the kittens that fascinated us and we plotted how we could borrow one of them for a plaything. Finally I got up the nerve one day to call through the fence to one of the Roberts girls. When I asked her for one of the kittens, she said, "sure", and tossed one of the poor things over the fence into our outstretched arms. Finding the coast clear at Elaine's apartment we hurried inside with our prize. Elaine got out her doll buggy and doll clothes to put on the unhappy clawing and squirming kitten. The kitten was old enough to have a mind of its own and it lashed out angrily at our efforts to control it. The wild creature slashed a deep scratch the length of Elaine's arm with its claws and sank its teeth deeply into my ring finger, releasing a gush of blood. Peggy fled out the front door, leaving it open. The cat leaped from my arms and dashed out behind her. Elaine and I went screaming for help. When my mother saw the blood streaming from my finger she took me home for first aide and then asked a neighbor with a car to drive us to Dr. Mitchell's office. It took four stitches to close the wound and I came home a very subdued eleven year old.

This was not to be the end of the incident, however. After the cat escaped from us, it returned to its home where it had a fit, biting three of the Roberts kids who were trying to subdue it. The wild cat broke free from them and jumped to the porch roof. From there it sprang to a window ledge, and with another leap landed on the sloping house roof. Still in a frenzy it jumped from the roof to the chimney top, lost its balance and fell down the chimney. The Fire Department was called and they retrieved the cat from the fireplace ashes where it had been knocked out by the fall. Since it was still breathing they put it in a cage and took it to the animal pound for 30 days observation for rabies. On the twenty-ninth day the cat died, and tests showed it had died from rabies. The next day an animal control officer called at the Roberts, Petersen and Stevens households to give us the bad news. All five of us, injured by the cat, were told we should have rabies shots. The Roberts were too poor to afford the treatments and the welfare department took over their case. Elaine's parents were Christian Scientists and flatly refused to let her receive treatment. My parents were too proud to accept charity and sacrificed in other areas in order to find the money necessary to pay for my shots.

For one full month my father drove me each evening to Dr. Mitchell's office where the doctor faithfully showed up to administer a shot of serum into my stomach. The shots were extremely painful, but I never cried or complained, I felt too guilty over what I had done and was thankful my parents had not punished me. Quite frankly, I think they were terrified that I would die. That idea never entered my confident eleven year old mind.

Elaine's arm healed, leaving a long white scar. She survived without getting rabies shots and the members of her church attributed this to their prayers. Staunch faith had protected her from the deadly infection. The Roberts family packed up and moved in the midst of the treatment period; I assume the children survived the ordeal. A few days after they left, an elderly couple moved into their house. From my bedroom window I watched them for days hauling out trash and debris. The Roberts' dogs and cats were abandoned when they moved, and some of the neighborhood kids joined the round up with the animal control officer. I wasn't one of those kids; instead I sat at my second story bedroom window watching the excitement and wondering what life still had to offer me.

Chapter 3

As days passed into weeks, my deep moods worried my parents. One day at the dinner table they dangled the idea of buying a pet canary. This was very appealing to me, and the next weekend we visited the neighborhood pet shop on Main Street. There I fell in love with a deep yellow, male canary who seemed to take a great interest in me when I singled him out from the other birds in the cage. My parents were stunned by the cost of all the equipment this small creature required. We had to purchase a cage, bird bath, cuttle-bone, papers and gravel for the bottom of the cage and regular bird seed plus special bird seed treats in ball form. These were major expenses for my unemployed father, but he rose to the occasion and counted out the dollars all these items cost.

We named the bird "Fluffy". He was an intelligent little thing and I soon had him coming out of the cage on my finger to get tasty food treats from between my lips. He quickly learned to get out of his cage door and fly all over the apartment. He experienced the usual calamities that befall captive birds. He burned his feet trying to land on a hot stove and nearly got a broken wing when a slamming door caught his wing tip. He even flew out an open window and fluttered through several neighborhood yards before we found him in a thoroughly exhausted condition.

Fluffy became a very spoiled and much indulged pet. My usually fastidious parents even allowed him on the dining room table at dinner time. He would hop from dish to dish, looking for the foods he liked. He'd grab what he wanted in his beak and proceed to make messes on the table as he snipped away at the food.

I developed a habit of getting him to hop on my finger so I could bring him close to my face. I loved the feel of his soft feathers against my cheek. I'd tell him to kiss me and he'd peck away at my face and lips. One day he was pecking at my face and accidently pecked the retina of my left eye. The vision in my eye blurred and I let the bird fly away as I ran for help from my mother. She was busy in the kitchen cooking dinner, but immediately stopped everything to examine my eye. She could see it was injured, and since it was too late in the day to reach my eye doctor at his office, she called Dr. Soper at his home.

When my father arrived home he found the household in turmoil. Dr. Soper wanted me taken to the emergency ward

Chapter 3

of Evanston Hospital for treatment. Daddy told my hysterical mother to stay home and finish preparing dinner, assuring her that I would be just fine. As my father and I were leaving the apartment my mother grabbed me and asked why I hadn't been wearing my glasses? I had to sheepishly own up to the fact that I had broken the rims again and couldn't wear them. If I'd had them on, Fluffy would not have injured me.

Dr. Soper had to close the wound in my eye with tiny delicate stitches. He warned that there was a strong probability that scar tissue would form and permanently blur the vision in that eye. This was a frightening possibility for my parents to accept. That evening they had a big argument over Fluffy's future. It took a real crying scene on my part to keep them from putting Fluffy to sleep. They gave in because crying was very bad for my injured eye.

Like a cat with nine lives, I once again survived a perilous accident brought on by an animal friend. My eye did heal OK and I regained normal vision, as the incident faded from our minds. Fluffy remained a faithful pet until my senior year in college, when he died quietly in his sleep. My grieving parents called me long distance at Carleton College, Minnesota, to tearfully tell me of his demise.

Harriet S. Wymbs

Cat on the Cay

Chapter 4

At Carleton College I made a lot of wonderful friends. One of them was a large moon faced girl who reminded me of a grown up Betty Ladd. Strangely enough my new friend was also a Betty and her family lived on a "gentleman's" farm in the Libertyville area of northern Illinois.

I loved to visit the Hall farm. They still kept egg laying chickens and a few farm animals in the restored barn. They had lots of beautiful cats they were always trying to give away; naturally I was vulnerable to the idea. Temptation caused me to succumb one day while visiting the farm with a friend. The half grown kitten I chose was a black and gray striped male, who was very nasty during the ride home.

My mother was less than enthusiastic when I walked into the house with my newly acquired cat, Misty. She had to finally give in to my argument that our new home in a quiet residential area of north Evanston was ideal for a cat. Traffic on the streets was light and the neighborhood was too expensive for families with young children who would tease a cat.

The very next day, after a restless night with a nervous cat who resented being housebound, Misty and I visited a nearby vet. Misty endured the necessary shots and got a reprieve from neutering because he was too young. In the ensuing weeks, Misty, the ex farm cat, displayed his love for freedom. The only time he showed up at our house was at meal time. We had no idea where he went or what he did between feedings, but one thing was certain, he knew we were his meal ticket. My efforts to tame him and show him the affection I felt were ignored with disdain. Misty was indifferent to human emotions.

In September I went off to Belvidere, Illinois to teach art in their public school system. My parents were stuck with an unfriendly cat they really didn't like or want. I wasn't surprised when, a few weeks later, my parents told me that Misty had disappeared completely. It was a whole year later before our next door neighbor admitted he had shot the cat in his garage because it was a constant nuisance.

Chapter 5

My experience with Misty was a poor start for a person who wanted a lasting relationship with a pet cat. I didn't have time to dwell on my disappointment as the United States was plunged into World War II in November of that year.

Despite the disruption of the war years, my life went on from teaching, to marriage, and then child rearing. When my parents moved to a new and larger home in Glenview, Illinois, they gave their Evanston home to my husband and me and our two children.

One Saturday morning I got a call from my excited mother. She had a stray cat locked in her garage that she thought would make a great pet for our children (Ellen was now four and Paul six years old). Mother said that the cat had been staying in their yard for several days and was very friendly and anxious to move in with them. Naturally she couldn't go along with that because she didn't want cat hair on her new furniture and rugs. She was sure a family from the nearby Naval Station had abandoned the cat when they had to move. She felt so sorry for the cat that she was determined to hold it prisoner until we came to see it.

Ellen and Paul were so excited about the prospects of a pet cat that we had to drive to Grandma's immediately. When we got there we found the biggest red tomcat any of us had ever seen. He was full of charm and purrs and his every move and facial expression told us he wanted to belong to our family. Paul gathered him up in his arms and we marched back to our car without a doubt about our decision.

Before the day was over we had chosen the name, Rusty, for our new family member. He accepted and responded to the name as though he had always known it; perhaps he had! Rusty's previous upbringing had been the best. He knew all the do's and dont's of house living.

We would have preferred a cat who stayed in at night, but Rusty would have none of it. He liked to start his nights on Paul's bed, until around midnight when he got restless and tried to get Paul to let him out. Paul was terrified of the dark, however, and wouldn't budge to accommodate the animal. In frustration, Rusty got into the habit of coming to us for help. Except on the coldest or rainiest nights, Rusty would spring onto our bed and sniff our faces until one of us reluctantly got up and let him out. Without fail he would be on the doorstep waiting for his breakfast in the morning.

Chapter 5

Rusty was scarcely accustomed to his new home in Evanston when Norm changed jobs and we bought and moved into a newly built home in Western Springs, Illinois. It was a wild 25 mile trip in the car from our old home to the new one. We managed to make it though, with the children and cat intact.

Our new home was in a fresh subdivision that still had open farm fields behind the back yard. Rusty thought he had moved to Heaven! He displayed his hunting expertise by bringing home a variety of game. Some of the rabbits were almost as big as he was. He always deposited his 'kills' at the front door so Norm couldn't help but trip over them when he went out to pick up the morning paper. Since Rusty was well fed, he never ate his catch of the day, bringing them home was his way of sharing the bounty with his family.

Rusty was a master student of human character, he knew Paul and I were cat people and Ellen and Norm were indifferent. He loved to sleep on Paul's bed and snuggle up close. Paul had terrible allergies and Rusty's fur gave him a constant runny nose. We tried to discourage them sleeping together, but it was a losing battle, Paul and the cat were inseparable pals. Rusty also adored me and I could never sit down to read or sew without him joining in. No matter what I had on my lap, he'd jump up and make me adjust to the situation.

Ellen was very open in her distaste for Rusty. If he sneaked into her room when she left her door open, she would kick him out and slam the door, hoping to catch his tail as he fled. Although he knew what kind of reception he would get from Ellen, Rusty treated it as a game of chance he liked to play. A few stolen minutes of pleasure in her room were worth all the risks he had to take!

Rusty and Norm never had a confrontation, they simply ignored each other. Once in a while when Norm fed Rusty, the cat would rub against his legs in a half hearted attempt to say "thank you". Occasionally Rusty tried to sneak a nap on Norm's and my bed. Caught in the act, he'd jump off and sneak away with a crafty expression on his face. I could imagine him saying, "I know it isn't you who objects, it's him!".

Both Paul and I suffered from terrible allergies and we knew that cat hair was one of our worst problems. We never brought up the subject because we wanted to keep Rusty. Paul's pediatrician had a different opinion. He said something had to be done to improve the boy's condition and that something was to get rid of the cat. After a heated family discussion we agreed we couldn't part with Rusty, the only solution was to turn him into an outdoor cat. When we let Rusty out for the night, we resolved that he would never come into the house again.

The next morning when Norm opened the door to get the paper he had to fight off a determined cat who wanted to get inside. Later, when we put the food and water dishes outside on the front stoop, Rusty was gone. We discovered him at the back of the house staring through the big picture window in the living room. He was hunched there against the glass with his fur blowing in the brisk fall wind. As we stooped down on

Chapter 5

the inside to talk to him, he meowed pitifully and tears came to our eyes.

The children had to go off to school and Norm to work. I was left alone to worry about Rusty. I gathered up his food dishes and took them to him, but he refused to eat. He followed me back to the door, demanding to be let in. I felt like a traitor when I squeezed inside the door, refusing him entrance.

When the children returned from school I was feeling wretched. Paul insisted on staying outside with Rusty. The weather was cold and threatening rain, but he was still with his cat when Norm returned home from work. Norm insisted that the boy come into the house. Paul's voice was husky and his nose was running. We didn't know whether it was a cold, an allergy or a reaction to the cold weather.

By evening it was obvious Paul had the flu, his temperature was mounting and he ached from head to foot. He stubbornly refused to go to bed and sat by the living room window sharing his misery with the pitiful cat on the other side. To resolve the problem, Norm went outside, picked up Rusty and brought him into the garage. We made a bed for the cat and put his food and water nearby. Paul was satisfied with this solution and finally went to bed.

It was fortunate that our bedrooms were at the front of the house and we couldn't hear Rusty wail all night. When we went to the kitchen in the morning we could hear his frantic cries through the garage door. When Norm let him out into the cold morning air, he raced from his prison and headed around the house. He found Paul's bedroom and managed to spring up to a window ledge and settle his bulk on the narrow shelf. When Paul saw him he started to bellow and announced that if the doctor wouldn't let Rusty back into the house he was never going to get well! He climbed back into his bed, turned his face to the wall and refused to talk to us.

Later in the morning I called the doctor and explained our dilemma. The doctor told me to wrap Paul in blankets and drive him to the office. Paul absolutely refused to cooperate and I was forced to ask the doctor to make a house call after hours. The doctor didn't get to us until dinner time. When he saw our disarray and Paul's sorrow, he was forced to change course. A boy with allergies was better than a dead boy; he told us to let Rusty back in.

By the next day, our household was back to normal, Paul's temperature was going down, Rusty was following his accustomed routine and we were a happy family again.

As Paul grew older he developed an intense interest in snakes, camelians, iguanas and alligators. By the age of eleven he was a real authority on these creatures. He kept a huge glass cage in his room for the iguanas and a smaller one for the camelians. In the basement he had his caged snakes and an aquarium for the baby alligators.

Rusty showed no interest in Paul's creatures, seeming to know that iguanas and snakes could get very mean when approached too closely. Quite often the snakes would get lost for days before we would locate them. If Rusty knew where they were, he never made an attempt to flush them out.

Chapter 5

The year Paul finished seventh grade and Ellen the fifth, Norm and I planned a summer trip to Europe with my parents. We talked my widowed Aunt Ethel into staying with the children. Ethel had never had children of her own and didn't like animals of any kind. We really didn't attempt to prepare her for a household with so many strange pets.

For many weeks Rusty had been losing weight. Nothing we offered him to eat seemed to please him. We realized he was no longer a young cat and attributed his problem to old age. Paul and Ellen promised they would faithfully care for all the pet animals while we were gone.

Of course, the moment we left they forgot all about their solemn promises and Ethel found herself trying to cope with problems she had never faced before. She flew into a rage if Paul let the reptiles loose, so he was forced to keep them caged. Rusty's problems weren't as simple. He was a sick cat and getting worse day by day. He could no longer control his bladder and the odor of his urine was everywhere in the house. No sooner would Ethel find, and clean up one spot, when he'd be leaking his bladder somewhere else. In desperation she made Paul carry Rusty to the basement. The poor animal lived out the rest of the month we were gone down in the dampness and gloom.

We returned home to find Rusty asleep on a pile of rags in the basement. He was skin and bones and barely roused when we touched him. The next morning after the family left for school and work, I wrapped a towel around Rusty's frail body and carried him to the car for the trip to the veterinarian. The doctor told me Rusty was dying of leukemia and should be put to sleep immediately. I gently handed him to one of his assistants and left quickly before I burst into tears.

When I got home I had a good cry and prepared myself to tell the family what had happened. Rusty had been a good and faithful member of our family and I felt terrible that in his last weeks of life we had deserted him when he most needed human love and understanding. How awful he must have felt, lying in that basement alone and frightened!

I forced myself to go down to the basement and clean up the foul smelling area where Rusty had lived out his last days. I felt that was the least I could do before the family came home asking about him. My answer was going to be, "He's gone to cat heaven."

Chapter 6

I was too broken up over Rusty's death to want another cat, but I was soon to have one anyway. Norm was half owner of a wholesale food business that supplied restaurants, schools and hospitals. Their warehouse was plagued with rats. The truck drivers solved this problem by picking up stray cats from the Chicago streets and bringing them to the warehouse. The cats got a good place to live , in return for catching the rats. No attempt was ever made to tame these warehouse cats, they were workers earning their room and board just like any other employees.

One morning as we were getting up, the phone rang, and Norm answered it. One of the drivers, already at the warehouse to load his truck, was very excited about what had happened to one of the cats. When Norm hung up, he told me one of the cats had an accident during the night and the driver wanted him to come down immediately, with his camera, and help the poor creature to survive.

Later that morning Norm returned home with a black and white cat in his arms. I couldn't believe my own eyes, this avowed cat hater was standing there before me, tenderly cradling a cringing cat! It was the wildest looking creature I had ever seen, its fur was bristled and its eyes wild, but it was making no effort to get loose. Obviously it sought protection from a world that had engulfed it.

As Norm caressed the cat, he asked, "Would you like to adopt this fellow? He really needs help." "Whatever happened?" I gasped. "It's an amazing story," Norm continued, "I got to the office and rushed into the warehouse calling for Tony. In the dim light I could make out his truck at the rear dock. With my camera ready I ran back and found Tony standing beside a cat with a broken glass jar around his neck. Apparently he had stuck his head into a mason jar thinking there was food inside. His head got stuck inside the jar, and in wild desperation he must have thrashed around until the jar broke. He got his head free alright, but he left a collar of jagged glass around his neck. The poor animal must have sat paralyzed all night, because any kind of movement would have meant getting his neck cut by the sharp glass."

Norm took some quick pictures of the animal; then he and Tony wrapped its head in a towel and broke away the glass collar. The cat made no attempt to resist their help, and when it was free it clung to Norm pitifully. His heart went out to the hapless creature, and deciding it needed something

Chapter 6

positive in its loveless life, he brought it home to me. Tony was in agreement, figuring it wouldn't be much of a rat catcher around the warehouse after it's harrowing night.

At first the children couldn't believe we had taken in another cat. What a strange animal it was, with short hind legs, scrawny body, bristly fur and demeaning attitude. It took days to get it to overcome its shyness and accept our attentions. The children, befitting its appearance, named him "Tramp".

Tramp was a young adolescent who was growing rapidly. He needed lots of good food and loving care. These ingredients, of course, were plentiful at our house. He successfully transformed Norm and Ellen into cat people and showed a preference for their company.

One day we realized that Tramp had developed into a beautiful, silky furred adult cat who needed a nicer name. We unanimously agreed to change "Tramp" to "Scamp" because our new friend had blossomed into a happy playful cat. His hind legs never lengthened in proportion to his front legs so he couldn't spring and climb like a normal cat. Ellen got an old towel and spread it on her bed. When Scamp looked like he wanted to sleep on her bed, she'd pick him up and plump him on the towel. He'd settle down and sleep most of the day, sometimes he'd still be there when she got home from school.

Scamp showed no more interest in Paul's reptiles than Rusty had. He was a Milquetoast sort of cat who never looked for challenges. He never stayed out overnight, preferring to curl up somewhere in the house.

When we decided to move to Florida in 1965 we naturally assumed that Scamp would adjust to the three day auto trip inside the roomy carrying case we had purchased.

It was late March, but a surprise snow storm hit the area the night before we were prepared to leave. To our amazement Scamp demanded to be let out that night. We were reluctant to let him go out, but he refused to be dissuaded. Norm got up several times during the night to see if Scamp wanted back in, but was disappointed each time. In the morning we learned that we had received one of the heaviest snowstorms of the year. When we opened the front door, there was no Scamp waiting in the snow. We had to get out and shovel the driveway clear of snow before the moving van arrived for the furniture at 9:00 AM. While I supervised the movers, Norm and Ellen got in the car and went searching the neighborhood for our lost cat. They returned home without finding a trace of him.

We pulled away from our old home late in the afternoon and headed southward towards Florida, without our cat. Scamp had disappeared forever; none of our neighborhood friends could ever find out what had happened to him.

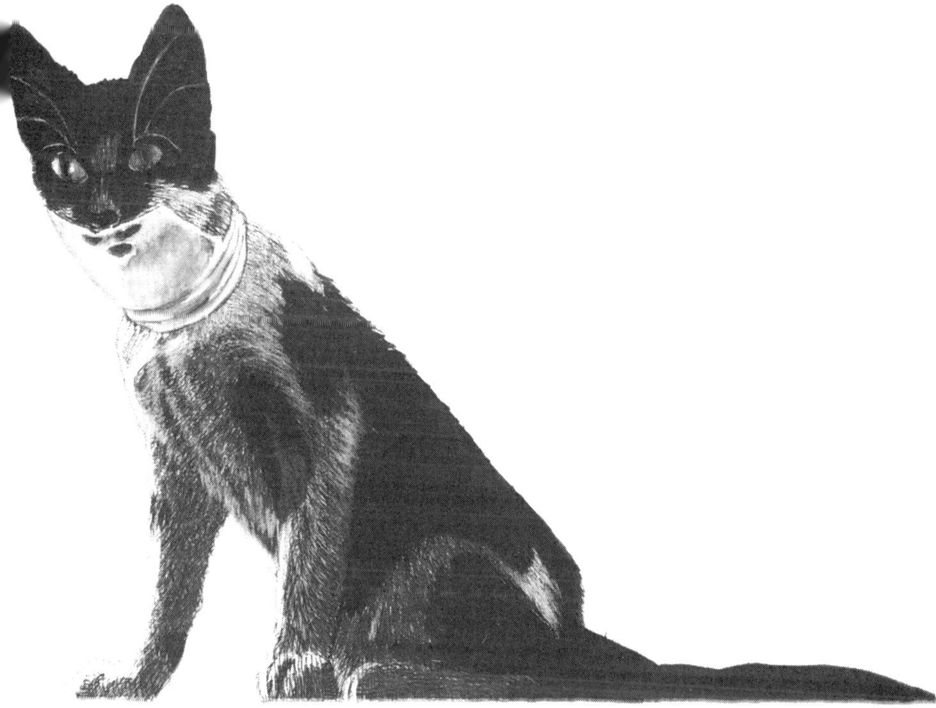

Chapter 7

After we were settled in our beautiful new waterfront home in Boca Raton, Florida we had many family discussions about getting a new pet. I was eventually out voted by a three to one decision that we should have a dog. Actually, the decision was made when Norm stopped by the Broward Humane Society. There he was won over by a small black male mongrel dog. He was adorable, even though he looked like he was made out of spare parts. He had the body of a beagle and the head of a pit bull, with the short legs of a daschund. Even as a tiny puppy he looked ferocious. He scared people with his snarling show of sharp teeth, then won their love with his furiously wagging tail and wiggling body.

When Ellen and Paul first saw him they thought he was Scamp reincarnated as a dog. They pointed out that his back legs, just like the original, were so short he couldn't jump properly. He simply had to be named Scamp, we all agreed.

This marvelous little dog lived up to his name for the next thirteen years, and the story of his life could fill a book. He was the heart and soul of our family, wherever we went, he traveled with us. During our years as avid boat owners, and later as seaplane advocates, he traveled with us on our frequent trips to the Bahamas.

Eventually our love for the Bahamas, most especially, Cat Cay, located in the Bimini chain, led us to purchase the old water plant on that beautiful island. The old stone and concrete tower, with its two one story wings, sat on a rocky peninsula jutting into the Atlantic Ocean. It took us three years, with native craftsmen, to turn the 1933 structure into a beautiful home with the look of a miniature Scottish Castle. People on the island referred to it as the Tower House, and the name was perfect.

The center of the tower was three very high stories tall. We had a graceful oak spiral staircase built in Miami and reassembled in Tower House to reach the upper floors.

Scamp learned to waddle up and down the spiral staircase without mishap. He adjusted to every facet of island living, except swimming in the ocean. He hated water his entire life, and bathing him was a nightmare.

During all the years Scamp came to the island with us we never thought much about why this island was called Cat Cay

Chapter 7

and the symbol for the island was a cat on a key. We hadn't realized that the presence of Scamp had prevented us from learning one of the island's secrets. It wasn't until after his death that the secret slowly unfolded.

As we drove our electric golf cart (automobiles are not allowed on the island) across the island on our first visit since Scamp's passing, we noticed the shadowy forms of cats peering at us from the safety of the wild thickets alongside the road. Once in a while they would dart across in front of our cart. They were small, scrawny animals with unusually large pointed ears. Their fear of mankind showed in their furtive glances at us as we passed. Later we learned that only in a few cases where kittens had been found very young and raised to be household pets, had these animals adjusted to humans. Most of the tamed cats belonged to Bahamians who lived and worked on the island. But, where, we asked, had these cats come from originally?

The explanations we got were as varied as the individuals giving them. Some Bahamians believed they had escaped from pirate ships that frequented the island waters hundreds of years ago. Since the old sailing ships always carried cats to control any rats on board, this explanation seemed plausible. One long time member of the Club on the island insisted the cats were introduced to the island for the purpose of restraining the rat population during the 1940's. He maintained the island was indeed named by the pirates, but not for the ships' cats. "Cat", he explained, was a rope used on a sailing vessel, this cat line was the origin for the name "Cat Cay". We were unable to accept this explanation, after all, the symbol for the island is a cat astride a key, not a rope around a key. The Bahamian story, a more romantic tale, is the accepted version.

One afternoon we decided to check out a house that had recently been vacated. As we approached the back stoop we noticed two cats perched on the rail. Both were pale red tigers, but one had much longer fur than the other. He also had only one ear. The cats didn't move as we got closer, and meowed pitifully when we talked to them. They were obviously pets that had been left behind to shift for themselves when the owners moved. The short haired cat was very friendly and let Norm hold him on his lap. He was pitifully thin and seemed eager to make new friends. When we were ready to leave, the cats resumed their places on the porch rail and watched us walk away.

Curiosity led us to inquire about the background of these cats. We learned they were rescued from a deep abandoned well where their mother had given birth. She had been able to spring up out of the well on her own, but couldn't get the kittens out. After the rescue, the kittens were tamed and became house pets until the family gave up their island home.

My interest in these cats was further stimulated when I bumped into the short haired red one on the beach the next day. It seemed strange to me that a cat would chose to roam along a sunny beach near the water's edge. It was early morning and the heat of the day was not yet unbearable. I was on my daily search for seashells and obviously my cat friend was on a search of his own. It wasn't long before a flock of gulls were diving for the tiny minnows that a wildly gyrating

Chapter 7

school of jacks were attacking in the shallow waters. The jacks drove the terrified minnows towards the beach and many flipped onto the wet sand. My new cat friend, unafraid of the gentle surf, rushed to the water's edge and made a meal of the tiny live fish. When he finished eating, he solemnly rejoined me and we resumed my search for shells.

We were nearing a small home close to the beach where I spotted a young couple sunning on deck chairs. They saw me approaching and called out a greeting. My cat friend knew them and left the beach to join them. The couple told me they had rescued Pooh and his brother Bonkers from the well. They had worked at the home and cared for the cats until the family had moved away. Now they had a new job at another home, but were still fond of the cats and fed them whenever it was possible to get food scraps.

I expected Pooh to stay with his friends when I returned to the beach and headed home. To my surprise, he promptly followed me and we walked around the bay together. When we got to our point, I scrambled up the embankment to Tower House. Pooh bounded up behind me and followed up the walk to the front door. Two and a half year-old grandson, Brad, was watching us through the glass door. He was squealing and pointing at the cat. When I opened the door, Pooh dashed past me into the house. Once inside he paced around our circular living room keeping a wary eye on Brad. He suddenly plopped down in the center of the room and let Brad pet him. Pooh and Brad became instant buddies, by afternoon when Brad took his nap on the couch in the family room, the cat jumped up and snuggled in next to him. In

33

Cat on the Cay

one short day, Pooh had taken control of our household. He didn't leave us until we were ready for bed. We were pretty sure, however, that he would stay nearby all night.

The next morning when the three of us woke up in our third floor bedroom, we could see a cat perched on the tiny window ledge of a small window near the top of the spiral staircase. Our immediate question was, "how did he get up there?" It seemed impossible that he could have jumped from the peak of the roof over the family room to this third floor window ledge, but there he was, plastered against the window glass on a shelf barely six inches wide!

Getting to his morning perch had been the result of sheer determination and some very accurate jumping. We wished we could ask Pooh how he had decided we slept on the top floor of the tower. Was it possible that he had worked his way around the building on the peaks of the roofs over the two single story wings, peering in the windows of the second floor bedrooms? The whole caper seemed impossible from our viewpoint, but the bigger question was, now that he was up there, how do we get him down? Norm and Brad dressed quickly and hurried downstairs and outside to try and coax him down. Pooh just stared impassively at them and made no effort to move. Norm came back inside to get some food he thought would attract Pooh. He held the dish up and waved it frantically at Pooh, but the composed cat refused to budge. Finally, Norm set the food dish on the patio and brought Brad back into the house. I had breakfast ready to serve when they came in and we proceeded to eat, wondering what to do next.

Chapter 7

Before we finished eating, we heard a cheerful meowing at the door. Pooh greeted us when we opened it, he had eaten the food on the patio and was ready for seconds. Each day we went through the same procedure. Pooh remained on the window ledge until we went downstairs to eat breakfast, then he would sneak down, announcing himself at the front door. We never had the thrill of seeing exactly how he got down from the third floor. The rest of our week's stay at the Tower, we looked forward to greeting him on the ledge every morning as we woke up.

During that week, Pooh spent all his time with us, with one exception, he refused to ride on our electric cart. Whenever we rode off on our vehicle, he settled down on the patio and patiently awaited our return. Walking was a different story. He loved to stroll with us on the beach or along the heavily shaded island road. Pooh hung so close to our legs that it sometimes hindered our progress.

Pooh enjoyed talking, as we walked along he would meow continuously with piercing intensity. Once inside the house he would continue the chatter, confident we understood every word! His conversation went beyond simple demands for food and water, or to be let out. He actually seemed to be communicating his thoughts to us. He never left us, or the house, without a long harangue; we figured he was patiently telling us where he was going and what he planned on doing before he returned.

As our visit drew to an end, we wondered if Pooh would return to his former haunts after we were gone. He was so happy to have found a family to replace the one he had lost, now he was about to lose this one too.

We were very sad when we flew away from Cat Cay in our seaplane; knowing that Pooh would be coming back to an empty house the next morning. How many mornings would he climb to the third floor window and look for us, before he gave up hope?

Cat on the Cay

Chapter 8

It was more than two months before we flew back to Cat Cay. As we taxied the plane up the boat ramp and parked on the landing area, a friend came out with some sad news. The Island Manager, she explained, had been ordered to kill off some of the cats because some key members thought they were overpopulating and a nuisance. Two of the cats killed were, Pooh's brother Bonkers, and the mother of the two of them. Our friend, Pooh, had survived because he apparently went to the Tower House that night and wasn't discovered.

Sure enough, when we drove up to Tower House, there was Pooh sprawled on the patio. He greeted us as though he had known all along it was just a matter of time before we returned and let him into his house!

Pooh was very thin and my first chore was to cut up some raw chicken livers for a tasty treat. After he ate, he left the kitchen. We were busy opening and sorting sacks of supplies which had to be stowed away in the cupboards and refrigerator. We didn't give a thought to Pooh until we finished our tasks, then we looked around for him. He wasn't on the first floor, so we started searching the upstairs rooms. There was no sign of him in either second floor bedroom and he didn't respond to our constant calls. When we got to our third floor bedroom, there he was, stretched out on a throw rug with a happy look of triumph on his face. Now that he had learned the wonders of the inside of our lair, he would never again climb up the roof to his perch on the window ledge. He was now a true insider who knew all the secrets of our domicile. He made it clear from that time on that there were no "off limits" in the house for him. However, since most of the interesting activity took place on the first floor, it was there that he spent most of his time.

Pooh wasn't much of a lap cat, but occasionally he would indulge me with the honor of his company. I observed that even when he was intimately happy in the safety of my lap and enjoying a gentle tickling, he never purred. This was a characteristic that held true for all the island cats we would get to know. Cat Cay cats, after hundreds of cat generations on the island, lost the art of purring.

Pooh was always ready for my early morning, and late afternoon walks around the bay. Whenever I squatted to pick up shells, he thought I was courting his attention. He would roll

Chapter 8

over next to me so I could tickle his stomach or stretch his neck so I could rub and tickle it. When I gently rubbed him behind the ears he would shiver with delight. Our progress along the beach was often slow, but neither of us cared, we just enjoyed being together. Sometimes he would suddenly dash up the embankment and into the thickets above the beach, completely disappearing. I'd just continue my beach prospecting and, sure enough, suddenly he would pounce down upon me out of the heavy undergrowth. It was a little game he seemed to especially enjoy. During the intimacy of those walks I realized that this cat, who lived all of his life on the island, mostly fending for himself in the wild, showed no signs of infections or problems with fleas such as had plagued poor old Scamp. His fur had a shiny luster and his skin was pink and clean. What a contrast to the misery suffered by our old dog on his island visits! In a matter of hours on the island, Scamp's fur would become infested with fleas that appeared out of nowhere. His Vet tried every medication known but we never licked the problem. It appeared the island cats had an immunity to insects and infection that visiting domestic dogs and cats did not share.

Our week's stay on the island passed quickly but I wasn't sad to be leaving. We planned to return shortly with Brad for a longer stay. I only regretted I could not convey this information to Pooh, so he'd stay near our home and away from future dangerous cat hunts until we returned. What I didn't know was that a neighbor who had just purchased a larger home on the north end of the island was also interested in Pooh's welfare. Before we returned to Cat Cay she caught him and took him on her golf cart to her new home. Consequently, when we returned with Brad, we couldn't find our cat. We were all depressed when days passed without a sign of Pooh the cat.

Norm had to return to the mainland on business and left Brad and me at Tower House for a week. Each evening, after dinner, I would get the golf cart out of the garage and take Brad for a drive from one end of the island to the other. We were up on the north end one evening when a red cat strolled out of the thicket just ahead of the cart. Brad screamed that it was Pooh, so we stopped and called to him. The cat galloped up to us and we had an emotional reunion with our friend Pooh. It was tough to say goodbye, and leave him behind as we turned around and headed back to Tower House. From then on we drove to the north end every evening hoping to see our old friend. Although we understood he was much safer from the cat hunters on that remote end of the island, that didn't help with our feeling of loss. Tower House was not the same without Pooh!

Cat on the Cay

Chapter 9

One of the few homes built on the north end of the island was up for resale. We were interested in buying a second home, so Brad and I went to look at it. The house sat on a large wooded lot, blending right in with the tropical growth as it was built entirely of mahogany. It looked huge with its four levels and wrap-around porches. As we parked our golf cart on the front walk we heard a loud meow. Then we saw Pooh sitting on the front steps looking like the master of the house. Brad had to go and pet his old friend before we made our inspection tour of the house. On the south side in the foundation we discovered a small door that flipped up revealing a large cistern under the lowest section of the building. It was full of water, and when I stuck my head inside the opening and yelled "who"; an echo came back, "who, who, who!" Brad was fascinated.

"Grandma, there's an owl in there!" He exclaimed.

"No Brad, that's an echo." I countered.

Brad stuck his head through the opening, along with me, and we both shouted words that echoed back to us. By this time Pooh had strolled around the house to see what we were doing. He sat there looking at us as though we were crazy.

Perhaps we were, for at that moment we both fell in love with this marvelous mahogany home.

When we left, Pooh sat in the yard watching us drive up the road, making no attempt to follow. On the way home, Brad suggested the house we had visited should be called "Echo House". We decided Grandpa simply had to buy it for us so Pooh could live with us once again.

The events of the next few months made this dream come true. We purchased Echo House in the fall of 1981, and when we went to stay there for the first time, Pooh was waiting to welcome us.

Echo house was built for casual living. Constructed of imported Philippine mahogany and cedar inside and out, it sat on a high bluff overlooking the Atlantic Ocean. The builder had carved out an opening in the jungle of growth just big enough for the house. The dense growth of tropical trees wrapped around the building, keeping it shaded and cool. Below the main building, in front, was a guest house.

Chapter 10

During our first prolonged stay at Echo House we realized Pooh had developed into a fully matured male. He began shooting small deposits of his urine on the furniture legs and walls of the house. It was his way of marking his territory and attracting females. Every time we caught him doing this we threw him out of the house and scrubbed the offended areas. It finally got so bad we had to deny him entry to the house. We even had to hose down the porch areas to get rid of the strong odor. Since his mating instincts were stronger than his interest in us, he wasn't offended by this stern treatment. During his short pauses for food, he was happy to grab a quick meal on the porch. His primary purpose in life was to lure a female into his territory while holding off competing males.

Most of his serious contests with challenging males took place after dark. Night after night the wild battles swirled around Echo House as Pooh looked more and more like a battered warrior. His ears became shredded and torn and there were many bloody slashes on his body.

The battle to end all battles came on a stormy night when lightening and thunder threatened our tiny island with a tropical deluge. We were awakened late at night by the wild screams of the cats. It was hot and sultry, and pitch black except for periodic illuminating flashes of lightening. We didn't want to get up and get involved in a cat fight, but Pooh's cries were getting desperate. Fearful for his survival, Norm bounded out of bed to investigate. I couldn't let him go alone, so grabbing a broom and flashlight from the kitchen we went out on the porch to assess the situation. The flood of light from the flash revealed Pooh and a huge pug faced male with long red hair embraced in a death clasp on the patio below. They were hissing and biting as they clung together, their sharp claws sinking into each other's flesh.

Norm rushed into the fray with his broom flailing and beat the cats until they broke apart and crouched a few inches from each other. He kept after the alien cat until he gave up the fight and fled into the darkness. We had a good look at the challenger, he was much heavier than Pooh and had none of the fox like features of our island cats. We wondered if he might be a domestic cat visiting the island. Fortunately for us, and Pooh, he didn't return to continue the battle and we all settled in for a good night's rest.

Chapter 10

Pooh participated in no more fights during the rest of our visit and he calmed down considerably. He became a more regular day time visitor, and apparently now assured of his territory, quit squirting inside the house. We speculated that he had taken a mate and must have her secluded somewhere in the wilds. We hoped the next time we came to the island there might be some baby kittens.

We flew back to Cat Cay in November of 1981 and stayed at Tower House. It was a very short visit and we only saw Pooh twice. He was saucy and fat, so we knew he was faring well at other homes in the vicinity. Although our Echo House was his home, and no other males dared intrude, Pooh was strong enough to fight his way into the handouts given to other cats at nearby homes. There was little doubt that he was now the dominant male on the north end of Cat Cay.

Harriet S. Wymbs

Cat on the Cay

Chapter 11

Our next island visit came in March of 1982. It was more than twenty four hours after our arrival before we first saw Pooh. He strolled up the back porch stairs, tail waving and greeting us with happy sounding meows.

He never seemed surprised to find us back home after long intervals. He simply picked up where he had last ended with us. Our visits always started with a demand for food, even if he wasn't hungry. Usually on his first day he would stay close by, taking long naps on the love seat and getting under foot while I worked in the kitchen. After he got used to having us back home, he settled into a less formal pattern of behavior. He would show up at odd times and only stay long enough to eat or reaffirm his friendship.

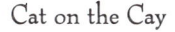

Remembering how Pooh used to love the beach, I decided to lure him down on our "new" beach. He surprised me again by showing he was already thoroughly familiar with it. We wandered along the ocean shore together for more than an hour. It was a sunny, warm morning and Pooh often sought cover in the sandstone caves along the shoreline bluffs. He would tuck himself back under the rocks so I could hardly see him. As I moved along the beach, he would wait until I was well past his lair, then he would bound out and playfully attack my legs from behind. Sometimes his enthusiastic play was too rough and he'd leave scratches on my legs. As I knelt to pick up seashells I also petted and tickled Pooh; he reveled in the attention.

We had reached a very wild and uninhabited area along the shore when Pooh suddenly sprang up the embankment and disappeared. I suspected he was returning to his mate secluded in the wild brush.

Pooh's mate remained a mystery to us until our July visit. We had arrived in the morning, but didn't see Pooh until late that afternoon. He seemed more nervous than usual and talked to us constantly. We sensed that whatever was on his mind should be of great concern to us. He looked steadily at us as he plaintively talked, his face expressing urgency. Finally he strode to the front door and demanded to be let out. We watched him gallop down the stairs, across the yard and into the thick growth beyond the road. All the while he was calling in his shrill voice. Suddenly, out of the woods emerged a small black and white female and three adorable kittens. When they reached the edge of the road, they stopped and sat blinking in the bright sun. Pooh emerged from behind

Chapter 11

them and, taking the lead, marched toward the house. The entourage hung close to Pooh, as if for protection. Norm opened the screen door and the whole family trooped into the house. I went into the kitchen and poured some milk into dishes and put them down where the cats could see them. Pooh, bursting with pride, led his family to the dishes and watched as they drank the milk.

Some confusion ensued after they had eaten and became anxious to get back outside. Eventually Pooh, with our help, herded them all back out the way they had entered. As they marched across the yard back toward the undergrowth, Pooh kept up a constant chatter and kept looking back at us. We knew he was assuring us they would be back tomorrow for another visit. With a new family member, we had to think of a name for Pooh's mate. I suggested "Missy Pooh". The named seemed exactly right for the little black and white mother.

When we woke up the next morning, Pooh was waiting at the sliding glass doors to our bedroom. We let him in and he settled down in his favorite spot by the ceiling length windows in the upper hallway. There he could observe the world around him and still be in position to intercept us as we came down to the kitchen for breakfast.

When we reached the lower level we discovered Missy and the kittens lined up in front of the glass doors to the living room. They were all curiously watching daddy Pooh striding around importantly inside the house. After getting out the cat food and serving it in its accustomed place in the kitchen, I opened the door and let the family in. The kittens

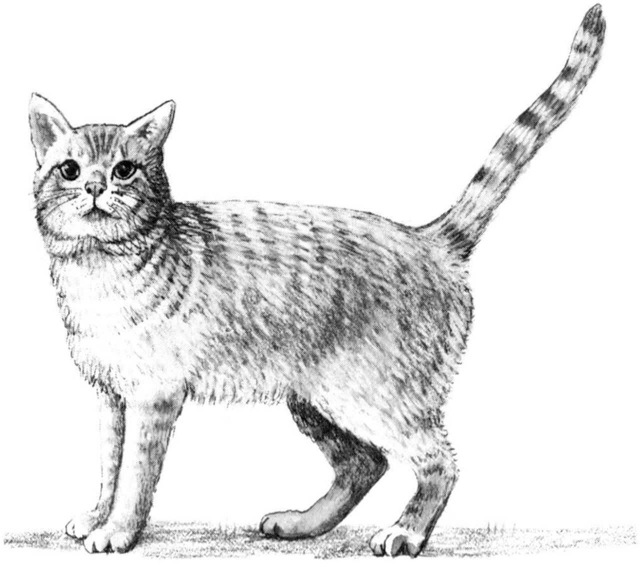

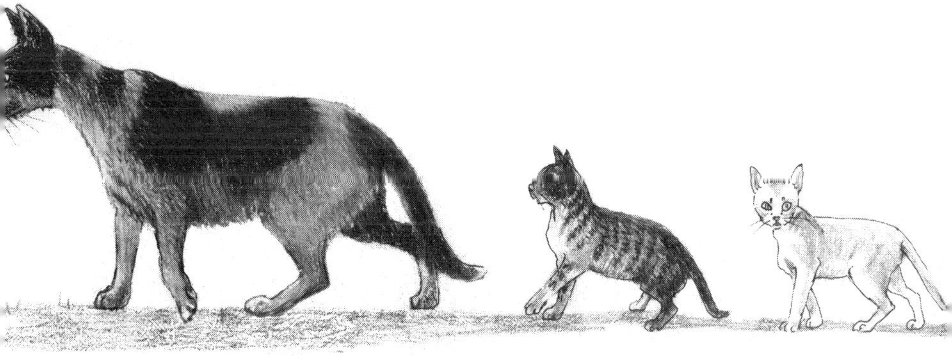

were squeamish and too excited to try and cope with dried cat food. They began wandering all over the house, and when we pursued them they ran under the beds. It was no easy task to push them out from under the beds with a broom and eventually herd them to the open door. We decided Missy and the kittens were too easily frightened to be dependable in the house. They would have to eat their meals on the porch. Missy was clearly upset over this arrangement. She meowed pitifully when we let Pooh inside and pushed her away. We finally gave in and let her have another try at inside eating. She stayed on her best behavior until the food was eaten. Not fully satisfied, she looked up on the kitchen counter and saw meat being thawed out for our meal. Like a flash she sprang up on the shelf and made a grab for the meat. I dove towards her and forced her to jump down before she completed her mission. Frightened by my reaction she fled through the open door. It was several days before she was willing to come inside again. The next time in, she succeeded in tipping over the wastebasket, scattering its contents across the floor. I had to scold her for her conduct and she left the house in a huff.

Missy proved to be a fast learner and never again did she attempt to get food that wasn't in the cat dishes. Unlike Pooh, she never hung around after eating. Care of her kittens was her first priority. They were lively little tigers in varying shades from grey and white to red. She was trying to wean them and get them to eat cat food.

All day long the kittens played on the porches. The days were very hot and the whole family would often gather in the shade under the stairs to the roof for their afternoon nap.

Chapter 11

The stairs provided a high perch where they could smell or see danger coming from any direction. They would lick and groom each other until they got sleepy and nodded off. The kittens always woke up first and would start teasing their parents. They would nip at their tails and jump on top of them until the older cats had their fill and snapped at the kids. The kittens would scamper joyfully in all directions to get away from their parents' wrath.

On cooler days the cats lounged on the soft cushioned porch furniture. The kittens learned to climb all over the chairs and tables playing their version of "king of the hill". They would try to involve their parents in the game; Missy and Pooh would endure their antics for quite a while before putting an end to the scuffling, nipping and pushing.

As the kittens grew older, the parents got sterner and expected more obedience and respect. We watched the kittens learn to stalk lizards in the tall grasses and jump to catch winged beetles in the air. It was obvious to us that the young cats preferred the food we gave them, even though the parents made them eat their wild catches. Never once did these cats go after the myriads of migrating birds that inhabited the island from time to time, nor did they chase or attempt to kill any of the wild turkeys and peacocks and their young that roamed the area. Years before these domestic birds had been set loose on the island to survive on their own. Over the years, as they reverted to a wild state, they learned to live in harmony with the cats.

We became so accustomed to seeing these kittens around our home that we assumed they would grow up to become a permanent part of life at Echo House. Before we left the island Norm built a feeder on the porch out of a large plastic bottle and pipe. It would supply dried food for the cats for at least a week after we left. Beyond that time the cats would have to turn to others on the island to feed them, or rely on their own ability to fend for themselves.

Chapter 12

Circumstances kept us away from the island for six months, not returning until after an extended trip to Egypt. It was late October and the weather was lovely, warm and sunny, but not humid. After our six month absence, we felt sure the cats would have forgotten us and moved on to a more dependable family. Several days passed without any sign of a cat near Echo House. Then in the middle of the night we were awakened by loud coughing and choking sounds at our bedroom door. The poor animal sounded like it was about to die. When Norm got up to turn on the porch light, there was Pooh huddled close to the glass door wrenching and coughing as though his very lungs were collapsing! I was certain he was having a fit and was afraid to let him inside. Norm felt we should try to help him and opened the door. Pooh tumbled into the room, quickly righting himself and setting out directly for the kitchen and his dish. There was now no sign of a cough and he looked his usual foxy self. He stood by his dish and demanded food in a loud complaining voice. He was ravenously hungry and seemed determined to eat us out of house and home at 2:45 in the morning! When he finally satisfied his appetite, he headed for the door, looking eminently satisfied that he'd accomplished his mission.

We went back to bed, but found it difficult to get back to sleep. Pooh's ploy had ruined our rest, but not our sense of humor. He had pulled a real fast one on us, and probably wouldn't forget how to do it again when the need arrived.

The next day Missy appeared with Pooh. She was heavy with kittens and we hoped she would have them before we left the island. She was quite willing to come into the house to feed, as long as she could stay close to Pooh. He patiently endured these loving attentions for a while, but then would indicate he'd had enough by snarling at her.

We always covered the love seat in the living room with a beach towel and Pooh knew he was allowed to curl up on the soft cushions for his afternoon nap. After finishing his ample meal, he hopped up to snooze off his dinner. Missy contemplated him for a while before jumping up next to him. She immediately began lovingly grooming him until he became irritated with the interruption of his rest and pushed her off the love seat. Undeterred, she jumped right back up and tried to snuggle down next to him. He became really angry and nipped at her. This was too much for even her to

Chapter 12

take, and she fled from the house. Unconcerned, Pooh yawned, rolled onto his back and slept until lunch time.

While I gave Pooh his lunch, Norm decided to take Missy's food out on the porch. He was determined to teach her to feed from his hand. The delicious odor of the meat bits were very tempting to her, finally becoming too much to resist

She dashed towards his hand and grabbed, getting the meat and gashing Norm's finger as well. He was stunned by the pain and bleeding and scolded Missy. She stood a few feet away from him looking truly repentant. It was then that Norm observed her clouded eyes and realized she had severe cataracts over both of them. The poor cat couldn't focus well enough to distinguish between his fingers and the food. After that experience neither of us ever attempted to hand feed Missy.

We had to return to Boca Raton before Missy's kittens were born. Six weeks later when we returned, the kittens (there were four of them) were at a delightful age. Missy was raising them in a cozy nest in the big wood pile under the house. They played on the porches as though they owned them, climbing up and down the stairs to the roof without fear. We could often hear them scampering on the roof above our heads. Missy hissed in warning if we got near her children, and refused to let us touch them. She taught them to stay out of our reach and under the wood pile when she wasn't around to protect them.

We were eating breakfast one morning when we heard the pitiful cry of a kitten in distress. Missy was on the porch nursing three of her kittens, who she pushed away as she perked her ears to the desperate cries of her fourth child. The wails were muted. At first we thought the kitten had somehow gotten inside the house. We searched under beds and opened closets but the source of the cries still eluded us. Concluding the young cat was not in the house, Norm began putting his ear to the walls on the side of the house where the cries seemed closer. The house had no insulation between the wood paneled inner and outer walls leaving considerable airspace between. We concluded that the kitten had found a hole at ground level between the walls and had crawled inside. Now, in the darkness between the solid wood barriers, he couldn't find his way back out. Norm stayed close to Missy as she searched under the center of the house which was built up on heavy stilts. As she carefully nosed around looking for the opening, she kept up a steady reassuring call to her trapped youngster. When she finally found what she considered the offending opening, she sat patiently alongside it for over an hour calling gently to the kitten. Eventually it worked its way back towards the sound of its mother's voice and emerged, terrified but unharmed.

 As soon as Missy had assembled her complete litter after that episode, she marched them off to the safety of the woods across the road. We never saw that family of youngsters again. For years after that occurrence, Missy raised all her litters in the depths of the woods. She didn't bring them to the house until they were in the last stages of nursing and she could draw upon our supply of cat food to wean them.

Chapter 12

Norm realized that such holes in the framing of the house not only presented a danger to future kittens, but also provided access to rats (rather prolific on the island). He sealed all possible access points, but Missy apparently was not convinced, as she kept her kittens away until they were old enough to keep their little noses out of dangerous holes! The rat problem was solved though!

Summers are very difficult for the cats. Very few people stay on the island from July until November. During that time the cats must supplement their diets with the natural foods available, like insects, lizards, rats and grasses. Some of the more enterprising, like Pooh, have learned to roam the beaches looking for minnows driven ashore by attacks of the roving schools of jacks in the shallow water. The cats work along the water's edge with ballet like dexterity, never getting their fur wet. At best it is a meager diet due to the competition of a large cat population on the little island only two miles long and three quarters of a mile wide at its widest.

Getting fresh water to drink is even harder than foraging for food during the periodic droughts. With no natural fresh water sources, the cats had learned to find small puddles under the brush, and even subsisted on the morning dew from the tropical nights.

As much as we loved these wild, sharp featured little cats, it was becoming obvious that they would become an unmanageable problem without birth control of some kind. Ironically, the people on the island were the prime cause of the population problem. Friendly folks, such as us, had been feeding the little creatures, creating for them a life of relative ease. Freed of their constant battle for the limited natural food supply, which had acted as a population control for two hundred years, people food was causing them to prosper and multiply like never before in their history. Added to their problem was the fact that more homes were being constructed on the island, reducing the available wild area which had been their natural habitat. As the growing cat population encroached more and more into man's civilized habitat, many of their natural habits offended the cat haters. There were many rumblings of anger and talk of retaliation against the cat population. Most of these complaints were ignored, but on the south end of the island an effort was started to eliminate many of the cats.

Chapter 13

I especially remember our July, 1982 visit to Echo House. We found Missy on the front porch with three languid kittens. Mother and children were pitifully thin. When Pooh turned up his appearance frightened us, he was so thin all his ribs showed and his wobbly legs barely supported him. He just flopped on the porch floor, closed his eyes and gave no response to my voice. He appeared to be near death, not only starved but very dehydrated. I went inside and got a bowl of water with a bit of milk added to it for Pooh, and a dish of meat scraps for Missy and the kittens. While they ate their food, I sat next to Pooh and dripped the liquid on his nose and mouth. He was forced to lick away the wetness.

I continued this ministering to Pooh for a long time and finally left the bowl of liquid at his side. Missy and the children moved in to claim the liquid so I was forced to bring them another bowl of the same mix. Before the afternoon was over, Pooh managed to arouse himself enough to drink from the bowl, although he showed no interest in solid food. It was the next day before he tried any real food, and then only in small amounts. I made a big fuss over him and kept him in the house all day. He looked at me with such devotion I wanted to cry.

When Brad and his parents arrived on the island a week later, Pooh was making a good recovery and was enjoying the role of happy house cat. He welcomed Brad like a long lost friend. It didn't matter how silly or rough Brad got with Pooh, he took it all in stride treating our grandson like a frisky kitten who hadn't yet learned how to restrain his actions.

One lovely bright day Brad and I decided to pack a picnic lunch and hike to a small park area near the north end of the island. As we started down the road, Pooh sprang out of the brush and joined us in his casual take charge way. This was familiar territory to the red cat and he was delighted to lead us to wherever we wanted to go. The dirt road tunneled itself through the thick growth which formed a green arch over our heads. The sunlight filtered through the canopy without the intense heat of the open areas, making walking a pleasure. Pooh kept bounding ahead of us, but before he got out of sight he would stop in the middle of the road and wait for us to catch up. Occasionally he would slip off into the heavy growth for a hunting trip, and then spring out at us like a tiger as we went by. If we jumped in surprise at his sudden reappearance, his face would light up in pleasure at his

Chapter 13

successful game of hide and seek. Since he knew the territory, and seemed to know exactly where we were going he turned into the little park ahead of us and laid claim to the palm shaded shelter at the ocean's edge.

We spread our towel on the cement slab under the shelter and opened our bag of goodies for lunch. Pooh stretched out beside us, his nose sniffing the sandwiches. We had cheese and peanut butter sandwiches and lemonade, all of which we shared with our companion. Pooh gratefully ate every scrap we offered, including the peanut butter which stuck in his mouth, necessitating a great deal of licking and fur cleaning. After lunch Brad climbed down the rocky cliff to the water throwing every moveable object he could lift, into the ocean. Pooh and I sat side by side in the coolness of the shelter and watched Brad expend his abundant energy. Pooh even attempted some feeble purring sounds to show his love and devotion. It finally proved that the island cats did have the ability to purr if sufficiently aroused by an emotional experience.

When we were ready to return home, Pooh resumed his services as our guide, prancing along in front of us, constantly looking back to make sure we were following. When we got near Echo House we saw Norm standing in the road. As he looked up into a tall gumbo limbo tree he motioned us to come and see what was happening. As we drew up, we saw Missy at the foot of the tree, her fur bristled and her body straining with anger. High up in the tree was a very unhappy black and white cat precariously clinging to a bobbing branch. Apparently this stranger had made the mistake of trying to move into her territory, and Missy had chased him up the tree in a frenzy of protective fury. She showed no intention of letting him come down from his frightened perch. The stand off continued for hours; but even after she relented and returned to her usual spot on the porch the intruder refused to leave the safety of his high tree limb. He was still up there long after darkness fell; but finally the next morning he was gone. For a cat with seriously blurred vision, Missy handled herself with swiftness and determination. Only her faithful mate Pooh showed equal fierceness in defending their home territory.

Cat on the Cay

Chapter 14

Whenever it is time to pack and leave the island, Norm and I load the cat feeder with dried food and fill their dishes on the porch with special food treats to keep them busy while we sneak away from the front of the house. On one trip our trick didn't work. Pooh was on the alert, refusing to be taken in by our obvious tactics. He knew we were preparing to leave and he was determined to go with us. He seldom sits on the front porch, but on that morning he was plastered up against the sliding doors. There was no way we could get out without physically pushing him out of our path. Norm told me to go out and pick him up and carry him to the back porch where the other cats were enjoying their treats. I tried it, all the while talking soothingly to him, but the moment I put him down next to the food dishes he dashed back ahead of me to the front porch! We were not going to be able to leave without him; he was triumphant! As we picked up our small traveling bags and stepped outside, Pooh was right at our side. We all strolled down the road together, Pooh was quite jaunty now; he had gotten his way and was confident he would find out what we were up to!

It is about a ¾ mile walk to the seaplane ramp and we knew that Pooh never went beyond International House which is about a ½ mile from our place. If he followed us beyond that point he would be in alien territory and could face real trouble from the well established "International" cats. We grew more and more concerned as we approached the big complex owned by Rockwell International Inc., and kept urging Pooh to go back home to Missy. He ignored our advice and joyfully pranced along our path. Finally we arrived at the frontier of Pooh's territory. The moment we crossed that invisible boundary, he sat down in the middle of the road. We stopped and said a sad goodbye to our devoted friend. Then picking up our bags we continued down the road. He sat unmoving in the middle of the road staring at our retreating forms. We could feel his sad eyes piercing our backs. Every time we looked back he still sat frozen on the spot, growing smaller as we moved on. We never experienced a more sorrowful departure from Cat Cay than that one.

Chapter 15

About a month later when we returned to our island, we found the house deserted. There wasn't a sign of a cat anywhere. The feeder on the back porch was empty, so we knew they had stayed as long as the food lasted. I placed dishes of special food on the porch while Norm refilled the feeder. We waited and watched for our friends for three days, but none returned. The fourth night Pooh showed up after we had gone to bed. He made such a fuss, talking a blue streak, we got up and let him in. He wanted food and nothing else, wolfing down the dried food we put in his dish. When I tried to pet him, he shied away. With his tummy now full, he wanted to leave.

The next day Missy showed up with Pooh, neither showing any interest in anything but getting three square meals. They had no time for their usual smooching with each other while in the house, all the while Pooh stared at us with real coolness in his eyes. We got the strong impression he still remembered being left in the middle of the road after our last trip and wasn't about to make up. Our new relationship was strictly formal, he wasn't going to get hurt again by getting too close to us. He knew we were fickle and would always walk out on him just when he was settling in to become a house cat. Over and over I tried to make up with him, but he just backed away.

Finally I got down on the floor at his level and butted heads with him just as Missy does when she wants to make up after a spat. Reluctantly he let me tickle him behind the ears. When I looked into his face, he had a sly, wise expression; I really felt that he was laughing at me. I guess I did look funny down on my haunches like a cat. Now that he had straightened me out, he was going to keep a close watch on my actions. Wherever I went during the day, he followed. Even though the weather was hot and the beach sunny, he trotted along with me on my afternoon trip for shells. When Norm and I took a walk down the road in the late afternoon, Pooh walked with us. Despite his earlier pouting, he couldn't resist rubbing and pushing our legs to show his happiness at having us back.

Missy was between litters, but, as usual her belly was swollen with tiny lives soon to be issued. Despite her failing eyesight, her other senses were so strong she could function like a normal cat. She was especially alert to every sound, movement or strange odor.

Chapter 15

As much as we wanted to be there when the kittens were born, it wasn't possible. We hoped she could get a sufficiently nourishing diet to nurse them properly. It was summer and there were few people on the island to provide food for the cats. She and Pooh would have to make do with catches of rats and lizards. Missy's summer litters were always the most vulnerable and some of the kittens died of starvation and dehydration. The spring and winter litters always did well, maturing strong and healthy.

We left Missy and Pooh with their unborn kittens, and didn't return to the island until the children were on the verge of becoming independent adolescent cats. There were three of them, and one was a black and white female. She looked very much like her mother and Missy seemed especially fond of her. During our visit, two of the kittens abruptly disappeared, the black and white favorite continuing to remain at Missy's side. They were inseparable during our stay, and as she grew to equal her mother in size there appeared to be no resentment or competition between them. Pooh was equally attentive to both females. Their threesome puzzled us, but it was not until our next island visit that we discovered why Missy kept this offspring close.

It was a shocking revelation to us when we found Pooh had taken his own daughter to mate and she now had three lovely kittens. Pooh was not as attentive a father to this family as he had been to past litters from Missy. He preferred to stay in the house and lounge on the love seat between meals. The kittens and their mother shifted for themselves outside!

67

Norm and I became concerned over what might have happened to Missy. Four days had passed and we had seen no sign of her in the area. Sadly, we thought her poor eyesight had done her in and her life had come to an end. Then, when we had become reconciled to her loss, she showed up at the front door looking healthy and plump. She happily came in the house and consumed a big meal without any of her usual signs of nervousness. After she finished, she went out the back door and contentedly flopped down next to her daughter and helped groom the kittens. That evening she and Pooh came in to dinner together. Pooh showered her with attention and loving nudges. Usually, in the past, it was she who drove Pooh crazy with her affectionate advances. Now the tables seemed to have turned, she wanted no part of his attentions and spit and snarled every time he tried to rub, lick or butt her!

The next day Pooh continued to court Missy and ignored his new family. Missy became more and more disturbed by his advances. All she wanted to do was love and groom her grandchildren and enjoy a quiet afternoon snooze with them. When Pooh continued to be an irritation, she nipped and scratched him. As he refused to back off, she fled from the porch and raced around into the front yard. Determined Pooh was off like a flash, chasing after his mate. Before he caught up, she dodged into a hollow in the base of a large tree near the road. We could see her sharp little face peering out at Pooh as he stood nearby appraising the situation. When he realized he couldn't get to her without facing her bared claws and teeth, he rose on his hind legs and clawed frantically at

Chapter 15

the trunk of the tree. Then he let out a desperate wild wail. It was a blood curdling expression of the depths of his frustration. He wanted his true love back, but she was having no part of him! Looking thoroughly dejected and broken hearted, he finally gave up and slouched off into the woods. As soon as he was gone, she scooted out of her lair and returned to her activities on the back porch.

We thought the happy union between Missy and Pooh was over forever. We went back into the house wondering if they would share or fight over the territory they had so long ruled together.

Harriet S. Wymbs

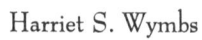

Cat on the Cay

Chapter 16

It was months before we returned to Echo House. To our amazement we found Pooh and Missy raising three kittens together. The daughter had disappeared and the old lovers seemed quite content with each other. Pooh looked like a battered warrior; his body had many scars along with some fresh gashes. His ears were torn and badly misshapen, looking like boxers' "cauliflower" ears. Apparently he had survived some hard battles to keep his territory and his mate. Looking back at the split up between Missy and Pooh, we wondered if she had just decided to take a sabbatical from kitten production. Perhaps her body was simply worn out or maybe she was just unable to conceive for a while. Whatever had been the problem, it appeared that Pooh had fought successfully to get her back, and now, once again, she was producing lovely kittens.

The battles Pooh had endured appeared to have sapped his strength. He was a very tired cat and relished with joy the opportunity to spend a few weeks in our house living in the lap of luxury. Most of his daytime activity consisted of trotting to the refrigerator every time I opened its door. He would gaze rapturously at the shelves of goodies, mentally sampling everything in view. He slept a great deal on the love seat during the day, and during the evening shared our snacks as he curled up on the couch next to me. As we watched television he occasionally jumped into my lap, something he hadn't done since those early days at Tower House. I noticed, as I held him, that many white hairs were appearing among the red.

Norm and I had no idea what kind of life span these island cats had. We figured that Pooh was now eight to nine years old. Missy was definitely much younger. If Pooh continued to be challenged by younger cats his strength would rapidly ebb. Some of his recent wounds were deep, vicious looking cuts. It made me wish we could take him back to the states. People who owned large boats often took island cats back to the U.S. with them. They could sneak them in because boats did not have to go through direct U.S. Customs inspection. With our seaplane, we had to clear through Customs as soon as we landed at Fort Lauderdale Airport. Without medical papers proving his U.S. Cat Citizenship, Pooh would have been impounded as an alien. There was nothing we could do to change his fate, Pooh

Chapter 16

belonged to Cat Cay and would live and die on its terms. His destiny, and that of Missy and their offspring was set by the limits of their island world.

Chapter 17

We always return to Cat Cay with mixed emotions, wondering if our cat friends will still be there or would fail to show up. Our next visit was typical, we flung open all the doors and windows hoping the cats were nearby and would hear. I even got out some frozen chicken so it could be thawed out and ready for their first meal. Like magic, Missy turned up and I was forced to put the chicken in the microwave oven so she could eat. She was quite casual about her visit and really didn't seem very hungry. She was plump and saucy looking and almost friendly toward us as she brushed against my legs. When she left we watched her walk down the back steps and join two black and grey striped males from her last litter. They were now fully grown and much larger than their mother. We had to admit they were by far the handsomest of Pooh and Missy's offspring. Sidling to either side of their mother, the threesome left the yard together.

After they were gone, Norm refilled the cat feeder. By the next morning most of the food was gone and no cats showed up at breakfast. By noon they were back sniffing at the back door. I prepared two bowls of food, expecting Missy to eat from one and her two grown children from the other. Instead, the boys deferred to their mother and watched as she daintily picked and chose the bits of food she wanted from both dishes. When she was satisfied and strolled to the end of the porch to groom herself, her kids moved in and finished the leftovers.

During the following days, Missy never came to the house without her lurking sons who seemed to be acting as her bodyguards. We could imagine what those husky cats would do to any strange male who tried to approach their mother! As the days passed without any sign of Pooh, we began to wonder if he was still alive. Whenever we took our afternoon strolls we kept a sharp eye out for any sign of his familiar red form. We never saw him and had finally given up hope of ever seeing him again.

One night we were sitting in bed watching a TV movie when we heard a familiar cat voice. There was no doubt about it, Pooh was back! I got up and opened the door. Out of the dark shot a wild looking Pooh cat! He was as nervous and jumpy as a mouse on the run, but he looked healthy and trim. He headed right for the kitchen and his food dish, keeping up a constant flow of chatter while I prepared his food. He

Chapter 17

bolted down the meal, constantly casting furtive glances around, seemingly concerned about his safety. He shied away from my touch and demanded to leave as soon as his hunger was satisfied.

Pooh only showed up one more time during our stay on the island. He came out of the night to demand a quick meal and then made another fast exit into the black jungle existence on north Cat Cay. We felt a pang of guilt that we could not offer him permanent sanctuary in our home. We believed that he was in his twilight years and fighting a desperate battle to hold his own against all the younger males he had fathered over the years.

He and Missy had created a large colony of offspring, who, in turn were busy making families of their own. These animals were now struggling to exist on the meager natural food supply available on the island. Only the strongest could survive through the off season when few people were on the island to provide supplements to their diet. Only the strongest could survive this existence and Pooh had lots of competition. It was obviously getting to be more and more of a chore for him to fight off all those spirited young bucks.

Hunger and thirst are very painful and can cause family ties to be torn asunder. None of Pooh and Missy's children ever challenged their parents authority under normal circumstances. Starvation, however, can turn animals (like people) into crazed beings. They will tear each other apart in battle for a scrap of food. There was no place for weaklings in this world; sickly kittens and elderly cats could not survive. Pooh appeared to be approaching the latter category.

A major change occurred on the island at this desperate time in the lives of the cat population. Dr Carl Maier and his wife Gail, who owned a home on the north end, and who were dedicated friends of cats, started shipping in loads of dried cat food. A Bahamian woman, who cared for their home and loved every cat on the island, was instrumental in starting this project. Rosa put large trays of food out every day for the cats to find. And find it they did, overnight the Maier's yard was filled with cats of every description, in numbers beyond anyone's belief. They came in all conditions to eat and recover their dignity. Some had been maimed in territorial or mating fights. Here they found genuine love and attention from Rosa along with a steady diet of commercial cat food and plenty of fresh water, extended with scraps she brought from the club dining room.

With good times beyond anything ever experienced before, the wild cats were mating and hiding in every corner of the little island to raise their new families. Kittens were popping up by the dozens. Unfortunately some of these new offspring were born with weak rear quarters and virtually useless rear legs. Trying to cope, they dragged themselves by their front legs to the feeding areas.
It was apparent that too much in-breeding was causing genetic disasters. When Dr. Maier discovered some of these kittens were also blind and couldn't function on their own after they were weaned, he had to destroy them. Obviously, nature had never meant for the cats on this island to be protected and fed to the point where the weak and maimed offspring survived babyhood. The island was rapidly

Chapter 17

becoming over populated with cats, many of whom were inferior and could not survive without man's help. The Maier's and Rosa's compassionate desire to help the cats was throwing the population out of balance.

The older cats, like Pooh, now had a place to find food when all else failed. He no longer had to fight frantically to save his territory at our house, because most of his competition had taken up permanent residence at the doctor's house. It gave Pooh breathing time to recover from his battle wounds and let his cauliflower ears heal. We were amazed to see our old friend start to recover his dignity and take on renewed vigor. This new lease on life did not extend to renewed superiority over his children, however, even though he tried to exert his authority.

One afternoon Pooh was slumbering in the shade on the porch when one of Missy's favorite grey striped sons came up to eat from the feeder. We called him "Big Boy", and his twin brother "Mighty Cat" because of their huge size. As Big Boy tried to sneak by Pooh without waking him, the older cat sprang into life and attacked his grown son. Big Boy, with no sign of animosity casually pushed Dad aside and proceeded to his destination, the feeding station. Pooh slunk back into the shadows, humiliated and crying. He looked so defeated and miserable that I took a special dish of chicken parts out to him, placing them gently under his nose. I gently stroked his fur as he ate and laughingly told him he wasn't the only one getting old and having to give in to the younger generation.

From that day on Pooh seemed to accept his new status as a senior citizen and he never again challenged any of his grown children who decided to hang around the old homestead. He could still sire new offspring and Missy worshiped him as much as ever. When a new batch of kittens arrived, he would become the protective father, snarling at any older kid who got too near the youngsters. In their golden years Missy and Pooh savored each new family they produced, keeping the youngsters close by until the next litter was ready for birth. As they mellowed with age they seemed to trust us more and more. Now, as we visited the island, they allowed the kittens to play around the house all day. There was one particular kitten that caught our attention because it showed no fear of us. Every time we left the sliding doors open for Missy or Pooh, the kitten followed them inside. It was cautious, however, and didn't go far beyond the open door most of the time.

One evening when the older cats insisted upon coming in for a late snack, the kitten slipped in behind them and followed to the parent's food dishes in the kitchen. When it attempted to eat from Missy's dish, its mother flew into a rage and pounced on her offspring with claws ripping into its fur. We jumped into the fray and scared Missy off. The kitten ran for cover under the sofa and refused to be intimidated, or to leave the house. I was snacking on cheese crackers and returned to the sofa to sit down. The kitten peeked out at me, looking so beguiling I offered it a bit of cracker. It accepted the tid-bit with enthusiasm and continued to eat whatever little treat I offered from my dish. Missy was too timid to

Chapter 17

challenge the kitten while it was near me, and moodily watched the process from across the room.

Eventually the kitten got nervous and sought the open door and freedom. The minute it got out the door, Missy and Pooh tore out after it. We heard loud squeals from the youngster, and then silence. We never saw that kitten again, I have always feared the parents killed it.

Missy and Pooh were willing to share the porch and outside area of the house in their declining years, but coming into our home was a privilege sacred to them only. After that night we never again permitted a friendly kitten access to the house.

Our seventeen day stay on the island ended on June 1, 1987 and we didn't return until August 3. Our grandson, now 9 years old, came over with his aunt and uncle (our daughter Ellen and spouse Gary) for a week's stay. With strangers in the house, Missy was very apprehensive about coming inside. After a few days both she and Pooh gauged their visits for times when Ellen, Gary and Brad were outside. Gradually, over the past few years Pooh had become less and less of a house cat. He would still let me touch him, but he refused to get near his old friend Brad. His main purpose in coming to the house was to enjoy the dining specialties, like fish, chicken and lobster scraps. Another family who had rebuilt an old house south of us were spending a lot of time on the island and Pooh had managed to endear himself to them. He was getting plenty of food at their back door, so much, in fact, that he was becoming downright fat! He was twice the cat we used to know, and although his fur was graying and lacked the beautiful gloss of his youth, he was still an imposing animal. I have never known an animal with a more expressive face. He could never hide his emotions and he always added emphasis with his talkativeness. It never seemed to occur to him that we didn't always understand cat language. By this time he had written off all humans as unreliable, taking advantage of what he could get from us without continuing the close ties we had once had. He seemed to understand his and our limitations and knew he could never become a full time house cat.

His life at this stage was that of a tramp, stopping at any convenient back door for a handout. He had detached himself emotionally from us, only occasionally forgetting and showing signs of friendliness. He never accepted my invitations to go for a walk up the road or along the beach. The only privilege he still demanded was the right to come in the house for his meals. Usually he took his meals at different times than Missy to insure he wouldn't have to share. Many times he showed up more through habit than because he was really hungry.

During the summer visit we caught glimpses of Big Boy and Mighty Cat but they remained deep in the shadows of the thick underbrush. The way the food disappeared from the porch feeder, however, we knew they came up during the night to eat.

Missy appeared to be heavy with kittens, but they had not been born before we left the island on August 12. By the time we returned on November 27 they had already matured without us getting a peek at them. Since we stayed at Tower

Chapter 17

House on the south end of the island, we only saw Pooh and Missy when we came to feed them at Echo House. We noted that Missy's eyes were so glazed over with cataracts that she must be nearly blind. Despite this, she seemed to still function pretty well, climbing with ease up and down the stairs to the four levels of the house. Perhaps she had memorized all the dimensions of her small world. When we are on the island Missy never roams far from Echo House, causing us to wonder if she ever goes with Pooh to distant houses for food when we are gone. Since we have never seen her perilously thin, Pooh must look out for her and take her along on his visits to the other homes.

Harriet S. Wymbs

Cat on the Cay

Chapter 18

The weather in February is never dependable on Cat Cay. The day we arrived it was warm and sunny. Twenty four hours later the skies had turned grey and the temperature dropped into the forties. We began to wish we had gone to snugly warm Tower House instead of big drafty Echo House. After having spent a day stowing away all the supplies and cleaning house, however, we were in no mood to move to the other end of the island. To fight the unusually cold weather, we went foraging for driftwood on the beach and built a roaring fire in the seldom used fireplace. Soon the living room was toasty warm and we were happy to seek indoor activities while the ocean raged, the winds howled and the skies dropped cold drizzling rain.

Missy showed up on the back porch the second day, escorting three lovely kittens. Two were black and grey striped and the third was a calico; none of them looked like combinations of Missy and Pooh. The youngsters were still nursing and not ready for solid food. They seemed familiar with their surroundings and happy to be on the porch, sheltered from the miserable elements. When Pooh casually strolled up on the porch, he and his mate indicated they were ready to come inside. The kittens lined up pressing their noses against the glass doors and watched their parents eating inside. His tummy full, Pooh, appearing to be his old self, decided it was a good time to catch some shut eye on the love seat. Missy returned to her young brood, spending the next hour licking each one from head to foot. The kittens glowed in this loving attention from mamma. When they were clean they all nursed until sleep overtook them and they flopped, one by one, in small heaps close to their mother's warmth and protection.

Mid morning, Norm took some small bits of food and tempted the kittens to eat out of his hand. One of the striped babies was excited by the odor of the chicken and kept sneaking closer until it could actually sniff the food. On one try it finally, delicately, lifted the food off Norm's fingers and gulped it down. Every day thereafter, Norm repeated the ritual. The calico kitten wanted very much to join in, but never overcame its shyness enough to grab the food, leaving all the special hand delivered treats to the striped sibling.

All three of the kittens learned to eat the dried food from the feeder before the end of the week. They seemed quite

Chapter 18

pleased to be able to eat whenever they wished. Missy frequently refused them her milk, no matter how hard they begged, rapidly weaning them to solid food. With a steady, and ample diet, we could see rapid development in these bright little creatures.

They furnished us with hours of amusement as we observed their good humored play. They climbed all over the porch furniture and had ferocious sounding mock battles with each other, replete with snarls, nips and artful pawing. No one ever got hurt but there were many tumbles to the floor when some one pushed too hard. Although the lighting was poor, Norm took a few pictures hoping to catch the joyful mood of their play.

After a week of dreary rain and blustery weather, it finally dawned clear and calm. We decided to take advantage of the elements while we could take off and fly across in our seaplane, so we packed to go home. Once again we said goodbye to another litter of kittens we had enjoyed and loved for a short time.

Chapter 19

Our arrival at Echo House on April 3, 1988 was a hectic one. We had chartered a sixteen passenger Chalk's seaplane to get us, our son, daughter in law, grandson and 450 pounds of supplies to Cat Cay. Brad had not been to the island since the previous summer and he was excited about seeing the cats again. Missy obliged him by showing up in the middle of the busy unpacking and restocking of the kitchen. Brad wanted to let her in, but I said, "Definitely not!". There was too much bustle and confusion and I knew she would get panicky. So she sat patiently at the door and we all forgot about her.

It must have been an hour later that I noticed her still sitting at the door, and told Brad he could let her in. She strolled past him, and instead of heading to the kitchen for food, started exploring the living room. After a thorough survey of the area, she headed for the lower floor bedrooms.

She was heavy with kittens and I realized she was looking for a nice spot to have them indoors. We didn't expect to stay longer than two weeks, and although we knew Brad would have loved watching such an event, we didn't have the time or facilities to handle the process.

It took all of us to finally corner wily Missy and direct her back outside. Brad thought the process was hilarious and added his own ten year old version of mayhem to the caper. For the rest of our stay, Missy was forced to accept her meals on the porch.

The next day Pooh showed up thin and hungry. For the past year he didn't seem to have been making out too well at the other homes in the area. Missy always seemed to stay plump and healthy. We often saw her catch and devour chameleons and we knew she also ate rats. Pooh hadn't been raised on these things and he didn't consider them proper cat food. He was overjoyed to find the porch feeder full and spent a lot of time filling up on the dried food. When we extended an invitation to come inside, he accepted and flopped down on the living room rug. In recent years we had become accustomed to his aloof attitude and his unwillingness to let us pet him. We assumed the wounds from his many years of violent cat fights had left his body sensitive to touch.

We were surprised when Pooh let Brad plop down beside him and start gently rubbing his whole body. The old cat stretched out and seemed to thoroughly enjoy Brad's attention. It was like old times when Brad and I would lie on the floor with Pooh between us while we tickled and rubbed

Chapter 19

him front and back. Even though Brad was now a big boy, somewhere back in his dim memories Pooh remembered who he was. Brad's friendly overtures and gentle mauling brought a positive response to their lifetime friendship.

Pooh stayed inside most of the day, fitfully sleeping or watching the household activities. He frequently visited his food dish making sure he didn't miss a stray goody I had dropped his way. After dinner he decided to join his family outside. From the next day on he was somewhat indifferent to us. He showed up at odd hours to eat and seemed quite happy to fill up from the porch feeder if we didn't invite him inside.

Occasionally we spotted the kittens from the February litter. They were quietly sneaking up to the feeder, one at a time. This infuriated Missy. When she caught them in the act she bristled and snarled and dove at them, snapping at their rears. They failed to accept her discipline seriously and kept returning. It was amusing to watch this never ending contest between mother and kids. Now that she was ready to have a new litter, she felt the older kids should leave the nest and make lives of their own somewhere else. They weren't buying her logic, especially when things were so good right where they were.

There was a new black and white male hanging around the house. He was fearful of us and kept his distance, but we could see that he had a great interest in Missy. She allowed him to hang around, but made it clear that Pooh was her true love.

Cat on the Cay

This cat was definitely not one of Missy's sons, he looked a bit like Big Boy and Mighty Cat but he lacked their forcefulness and dignity. His fur never looked glossy and groomed like the others, he really was slovenly. Day after day he showed up, spending his time down in the yard. We suspected he came up to the feeder at night when we couldn't see him. Pooh ignored him, tolerating his presence. We began to suspect Pooh could no longer father kittens and this strange male was the father of the next litter.

   We had to leave the island on April 14 before Missy gave birth. Her great bulk made it difficult for her to move around. We were sorry to leave her in such a state and hoped she and the kittens would survive.

Chapter 20

For the past few years my interest in the cats of Cat Cay has become more and more challenging. My observations have become more detailed and the chronology carefully recorded. It is always harder to remember details after the fact, especially since we have been involved with so many generations of cats.

We arrived at Cat Cay on Thursday, May 26, 1988. Our trip across the Bermuda Triangle was sparkling, the air so clear that when we leveled out at 3,000 feet coming out of Pompano Air Park, we could see the Bimini, Bahama, Islands some 60 miles away. The ocean was so calm we could have easily landed anywhere; our let down at Cat Cay led to a flawless, smooth landing on the water.

We had a heavy load of groceries and supplies to store away when we arrived at Echo House. Before we finished our routine, Missy was at the door crying to come in. She was pitifully small and her hunger was overwhelming. We had never seen her in such poor shape on any other trip. Obviously she had not been able to feed well at the Maier house. Over the past months the colony of 50 or more cats at that home had consolidated into a closed group and outside cats like Missy were not welcome. Missy and Pooh were too wed to their own territory to leave it and become regular members of the congregate living at the Maier's. Most of their offspring, however, had readily been assimilated into the large group down the road.

As Missy worked through her third helping of food, we observed that her breasts were full of milk. She seemed to be raising another family against extreme hardships. Once she was filled she wasted no time in getting out and disappearing under the house. Our next concern was for Pooh, would the old fellow show up once more?

By evening foul weather was brewing, the winds were churning the ocean into a white frenzy. Finally the heavens gushed forth torrential rains with wild flashes of lightning dashing across the sky. Deafening explosions of thunder burst overhead, shaking the very foundations of Echo House. We kept hoping the cats would seek refuge with us inside, but none appeared at the doors.

Morning came, cool and rainy, and we had to accept the idea of a day of indoor activities. It was late afternoon when old friend Pooh dashed up the porch stairs drenched to the skin. He looked dreadful; all his ribs showed and his legs were as thin as sticks. I had a lot of turkey and fish scraps

Chapter 20

waiting for him, which he devoured so rapidly he became convulsed with stomach cramps. Fearing he might throw up his hastily eaten dinner, I encouraged him to leave immediately. He was anxious to go, despite the miserable weather. Missy failed to return at all, leading us to conclude that she and Pooh were guarding a litter of kittens somewhere near by.

We had no more cat visitations until the evening of the next day. At dusk, Missy's black and white male companion showed up at the feeder for a quick meal. He appeared in much better physical condition than either Missy or Pooh, but still he ate hungrily. For a cat with such stout dimensions he still had a disheveled appearance and a lack of determination in his conduct. He always appeared frightened and fearful of his surroundings.

The next morning was bright and sunny and a more relaxed Missy and Pooh showed up for a meal together. Their good spirits helped them look much healthier than two days earlier. They put on a great show of affection for each other while I prepared their bowls of food. They still acted as though they were on the edge of starvation and demanded two refills before they were satisfied. They left together, heading for the thickets across the road, no longer dejected with their miserable situation. We were back and they knew that, at least for a short time, all would be well in their small world.

The next Saturday our daughter Ellen and son in law Gary arrived for a week's stay. No cats showed up to greet the new arrivals. The big surprise came on Sunday when I came down to the kitchen. There was a heavy line up of cats at the living room doors. Watching my every move were mom and dad and three young adult cats. I recognized Calico and the grey and white striped youngster, but the second striped cat was missing. Added to the group was a handsome red cat with a bright white bib. When I let Pooh and Missy inside the younger cats took their turns eating at the feeder. They had an established pecking order, the red cat ate first, then the striped one and finally the calico.

When Missy and Pooh rejoined the children on the porch, they all decided to stay put and not wander off into the morning showers.

With the weather cloudy, and frequent showers, Ellen and Gary were unable to take the Rubber Duck (our inflatable boat) out into the ocean. Gary spent the day fishing from shore, often in the rain, while Ellen and I puttered around the house.

The cats adjusted to this weather better than we did. Their family played and ate on the sheltered porch while Pooh moved inside to slumber in comfort on his love seat. He snoozed for hours without even twitching, but as soon as I moved into the kitchen one of his eyes would pop open and in a flash he would spring into action fearing a missed opportunity to feed. If I had to open the refrigerator he was there beside me peering with wide eyes at the wondrous contents. He would twist and wind his body around my legs, begging for another tid-bit. I had to utter a number of harsh "no's" to discourage him. Whenever Missy came in to eat, she too, was friendlier than usual. She didn't flinch when she bumped into me, and she stood her ground when I refilled her food bowl.

Since Missy and Pooh were accepting their adolescent offspring as permanent residents, we decided to give them names. We called the red one "Little Pooh" and the others "Tiger" and "Calico". Although Little Pooh held a preferential position in the adolescent pecking order; he did not show overly aggressive behavior. When it was time to eat, he went to the bowl and ate first, the other two were happy to share whatever he left for them after satisfying his hunger. When Little Pooh settled down to snooze the other two would approach hesitantly. If he remained passive they would happily settle in and sleep next to him. If he showed any sign of being disgruntled by their presence, they would slink off elsewhere for their naps.

In place of Big Boy and Mighty Cat, who had long ago disappeared, Missy now had her big mussy black and white escort. Until this time we assumed that Little Pooh, Tiger and Calico were a complete litter, but when her big escort was along they also had a black and white adolescent who hung in with the crowd. She accepted the young cat as her own and included him with the latest family, they were all obviously of the same age. However strange it seemed to us, we concluded that Missy had two fathers for her latest brood. Pooh could easily be matched to three, while the little black and white was the image of the extra escort. The adult males only showed interest in their own children. Pooh allowed the first three to maul and play with him, while the black and white daddy acted very protective over his little one. Missy accepted all four equally; they were definitely her kids. We began to call the two additional cats "Black and White Daddy, and "Junior".

I was so intrigued by the concept of two fathers for one litter of cats that I later did some research on the subject. I learned that a female cat is often in heat long enough to be impregnated by more than one male. When that happens, occasionally the females eggs will be fertilized from two different sources. Nowhere in my studies could I find anything that explained how the males could identify and relate only to their own offspring, as had Pooh and Big Black and White .

Along with Pooh, Black and White Daddy squirted the outside walls and posts of the house with his scent to establish ownership. The rains were at least good for one thing, they washed away the pungent odor. Putting up with male cat scent was one of the disadvantages of having wild cats. That drawback was offset by the fact we were no longer plagued by the hoards of rats that used to cause great destruction. These little beasts could gnaw their way through heavy wood siding and doors to invade houses. They chewed holes in rugs and upholstery, ate the labels off food cans, bit holes in plastic containers so the contents poured out, and left their droppings everywhere. As our cat population increased, the rats decreased and we realized they were furnishing a major portion of the cats' diet. We often saw our adult cats hiding in the fallen leaves, or under the bushes, never twitching a muscle until they sprang to life and grabbed a rat.

Within minutes, the kittens would zero in to enjoy a feast

of red meat with their parents. Only Pooh, who was raised in a more people oriented environment, considered this fare beneath his culture. With the increase in cat population there has been a corresponding decrease in the number of rats on the island, which is probably one of the reasons why they become so scrawny when there aren't many people around to supplement their natural diet.

Since the land birds, other than the turkeys and peacocks on the island, are migratory, the cats have never considered them as a food source. The sea birds, such as gulls, pelicans, egrets and the like, are either too big or too wily for the cats to best in combat. In all our years on Cat Cay, we have never seen a cat attack a bird of any kind. Members' dogs, however, who roam freely despite the island's leash rules, often attack and kill the adult turkeys and their chicks. Since they are all well fed and pampered canines, they never eat their kills, leaving them to rot in our yard where we are left with the smelly cleanup.

The day after Ellen and Gary flew home on Chalk's Grumman-amphibian, the sun came out and the breeze turned gentle. We packed quickly, closed down the house and headed for our plane and home to Boca Raton.

Chapter 21

We like to get an early start when we fly to Cat Cay, so we can arrive on the island by 10:30 AM. The day we chose in early August proved to be rainy, despite the official prediction it would be a fair day. Since we had guests arriving, via Chalks, two days later, it was imperative we make every effort to get there. By noon the weather was clearing and we drove to the airport. While checking the airplane, Norm discovered a mechanical problem that forced a visit to the big maintenance hanger for repairs. Gus and his crew went to work immediately, and at 3:00 PM we were able to take off over the ocean. Forty minutes later, after a beautiful flight, we landed at Cat Cay. The van was waiting for us, and without delay we loaded it with our supplies and headed for Echo House.

It wasn't more than 15 minutes before Pooh showed up at the front door. He was very thin and we let him in even though he was under foot while we put the supplies away. Having nothing thawed out, I dumped dried cat food in his dish. He batted me sharply with his claws, letting me know in no uncertain terms he wanted some real food, like chicken. I was forced to look up some frozen chicken parts and thaw them out in the microwave oven. Pooh ate several helpings of the gizzards, hearts and livers, then he topped his meal off with some dried cat food and water. I was afraid that his shrunken stomach couldn't hold all that he had eaten and worried a bit about having him sleep on the love seat. Taking no chances, I insisted he stretch out on the rug instead of the furniture. He lay there contented until he heard Little Pooh talking at the back door. He came awake quickly, rushing to the screen door and telling off the younger cat in angry snarls. He wasn't about to have Little Pooh finagle his way inside. The poor old fellow still considered this to be the one privilege only he and Missy enjoyed.

At dinner time Missy showed up. The porch feeder was filled, but she wanted equal treatment with Pooh inside the house. She and Pooh shared their dinner inside, with the usual amount of smooching between portions.

That evening Little Pooh showed up at the feeder and we observed he was turning into a handsome adult cat. While he was eating, a much larger pale red cat showed up and patiently waited for Little Pooh to finish before he

Chapter 21

approached the feeder. Little Pooh had his back turned, drinking water, when he became aware of the new arrival. Low menacing growls erupted from the depth of his throat, causing the large cat to scoot away until Little Pooh left. When the coast was clear he sneaked back to the feeder for another try.

Later in the evening Calico and Tiger emerged from the blackness and headed for the feeder. Norm went to the window and greeted them as they came over for a little cat talk. It is amazing how the word is passed from cat to cat that the Wymbs are back and the feeder is full. Between 5:00 and 9:15 PM the feeder went from full to half full. It holds over 3 pounds of food.

Wednesday morning we found Pooh and Missy at the front door, their grown kids had taken over the back porch. We let the elderly lovers in to enjoy the special privilege of eating inside. Meanwhile, Little Pooh, Calico, Tiger, Big Red, and Black and White Daddy took turns, in that order, at the feeder. The latter two were quite cowardly with low self esteem.

Mid morning I was busily cleaning our bedroom when Norm called me to the living room. As I came down the stairs from the upper level, he motioned for me to come quietly. Slipping over towards the front sliding doors I saw Pooh and Missy with two black and white babies. They certainly looked like miniature clones of Missy and Black and White Daddy, but it was Pooh who was playing the part of proud father! If, indeed, as we surmised, these youngsters belonged to Black and White Daddy, it appeared that he lacked the spunk or ability to stand up for his parental rights. Missy's choice of the big black outsider as a temporary partner had in no way challenged Pooh's superior position as the number one male in her life. If Pooh wished to claim parental dominance over this batch of youngsters, Missy and Black and White Daddy weren't going to argue with him!

All day long Missy and Pooh stayed on the front porch with their new family. They took time out to come inside for meals, but did so separately, so the kittens always had one of them standing by.

On the back porch we noticed a new pecking order was being established. Tiger now took over as dominant cat and Little Pooh disappeared for long periods. Tiger acted like a lookout, keeping a sharp eye on all activity, inside and out of the house. All day she challenged other members of the clan who came to eat. Those she didn't want around she drove off without argument. Several times during the day Norm cut up tiny bits of chicken and held them out to Tiger. The cat, tantalized by the odor, carefully approached the delicacies and flipped them from his hand with her tongue. When the last treat was gone, she licked Norm's fingers clean.

Pooh observed one of these events between Norm and Tiger from his comfortable perch in the house. He became quite upset by the performance of the younger cat and insisted upon be let out onto the porch. He went to the area where Tiger had eaten the food from Norm and licked it clean of the young cat's scent!

Chapter 21

In the meantime I put a dish of moist commercial cat food in a dish for the new kittens. Missy showed them how to eat, and urged them to try it. When they found it was easy to chew they attacked it enthusiastically and I had to bring out seconds.

That day I prepared fish and rice for dinner. Bahamian cats, like Bahamian people, love rice, so I made extra for our little friends. I had flavored it with cheese and herbs and it was an instant hit with the gang. Not a grain of rice was left in their dishes!

Thursday morning dawned clear and calm. Our cats had established an orderly life, with Missy, Pooh and the babies settled on the front porch and the rest of the cats on the back porch. Occasionally Black and White Daddy and Junior would sneak around to the front of the house and quietly watch Pooh and Missy tending the needs of the young litter. Finally, on one of these visits, Junior crept up the stairs and edged his way in with the kittens. Missy gave Pooh a warning look that held him from action. She then permitted Junior to settle in with the younger kittens who appeared to be smaller clones of himself. He looked delighted with his accomplishment and Daddy happily accepted this as an indication that Pooh and Missy were acknowledging his family line through Junior.

When our guests Arlene and her nine year old granddaughter, Beckie, arrived on Chalk's that afternoon, we warned them we had a lot of wild cats at the house. Beckie said this would be just fine because she had a pet Siamese cat at home that was real skittish. Beckie, like our Brad, proved to the cats that she understood them. During her stay the cats accepted her presence and never were upset by her coming and going. She took a real interest in their activities and became as involved in cat watching as we were.

Our earlier calculations on the amount of cat food needed proved to be far short of the demand. The cats were consuming three pounds every two days, so we were forced to leave the feeder empty for a while. This upset the gang and they became very vocal in their displeasure. Tiger was especially upset because she no longer had a purpose in life, there was nothing left to guard! As the day wore on, they all wandered away, looking for other sources of food. Missy and Pooh showed up at their regular feeding times with hopeful looks on their faces and we rewarded them inside with their usual fare. We didn't dare try to feed the babies on the front porch because the older cats kept a watchful eye on the house and would have forcefully claimed it for themselves. Knowing she must find another source of solid food for her little brood, Missy went off hunting in the underbrush. It was early evening, and Arlene, Beckie and I went for a walk. When we returned we spotted Missy with a live rat struggling in her mouth. From the secluded vantage point of the front porch, we watched her kill the rat and rip it open. She then called for the kittens to come out of hiding. Her little ones then received a motherly lesson in how to eat raw meat. The sight was too much for Arlene, but Beckie and I stayed to watch the whole affair. When Missy and the kittens were finally full, the remains were left for Black and White Daddy to finish. Between them, they devoured every bit of the rat,

Chapter 21

even the bones! It amazed us that Missy, with her blurred vision, could catch a fast moving rat in the heavy growth near our house.

Friday morning seemed very quiet. Only Missy and Pooh were on the front porch, with their babies, waiting to come inside for breakfast. When the elders came in, the kittens squealed plaintively and we obliged with a dish of soft cat food for them. All our other cat friends had gone elsewhere for their breakfasts. By afternoon they all straggled back, looking hungry and dejected. Norm finally relented and refilled the feeder.

Saturday morning the two black and white kittens showed up with the other cats at the back door. They had learned to chew dried food and took their turns eating at the feeder. That evening we had a lobster stir fry for dinner and there were generous leftovers for the cats. They enthusiastically attacked the dishes we filled, and ate every scrap, including bamboo shoots, broccoli, peas, onions and mushrooms!

Sunday was a rainy and windy day. Our motley array of cats huddled all day on the porches, languid and accommodating. Even Pooh remained quiet and tolerant of the other members of the family. Black and White daddy and Junior showed up at odd times to eat, and we assumed they were hiding out under the house. Little Pooh, who hadn't shown his face for several days was now back with the gang. Norm spent some time getting Tiger and Little Pooh to eat from his hand. This brought Pooh to life and he became very jealous and vocal. Tiger gave tit for tat, snarling back at him and chasing him under the upper porch. The old guy stayed there for a long time with an angry pout on his face.

Monday morning Norm and I were hanging out laundry and Becky was exploring underneath the house. She noticed little creatures moving in the woodpile and called for us to investigate. Looking closely we discovered two tiny red tiger kittens snuggled together in an opening at the bottom of a pile of lumber. Our voices triggered their curiosity and they started to move around while we admired their miniature perfection. Little Pooh strolled into the scene and settled comfortably in with the babies. The next scene really startled us, the babies were nursing! Little Pooh, the one we considered "son of Pooh" was their mother!

I had always believed red tiger cats were males. Now I was to learn that red cats with some off coloring could be females. Little Pooh had a white bib and white paws, and sure wasn't a male! Since her name "Little Pooh" was no longer appropriate, I re-christened her "Lilipooh". Until this new revelation, we had accepted Tiger as the female and Lilipooh as the male. Now we began to reexamine the personalities of the two young cats. While Tiger was the more aggressive, Lilipooh held her own through quiet firmness. Being unable to examine these wild cats physically, we had to figure out their sexes by observation of their personalities. With our opinions firmly reversed by the advent of the new family, we assumed Tiger was the male, and probably the new father.

Kitten watching became the preoccupation of our household. It was very difficult for Becky to merely observe

Chapter 21

and not touch the cute little babies. We explained to her that Lilipooh had placed so much trust in us that she was raising her children in a wood pile only three feet from our back side walk. Until this time, kittens had always been reared in hiding until they could function on their own, never had any of them been in full view from birth, such as this family. We told her Lilipooh would probably turn into the protective wild cat she really was if anyone tried to touch her babies. Becky realized she could be hurt by Lilipooh's sharp claws and teeth if she felt her family was in danger.

It took several days before we decided that a large red male, who sometimes appeared near the nest, must be the father. He never showed any particular affection towards Lilipooh, but he was always lurking in the area and sneaked up to the feeder at times when the other cats were not around. Pooh was getting very cantankerous during this period. He was squirting his scent all around the outside of the house and no amount of scolding would make him stop. His children often snarled at him and tried to get to the feeder while he ate, or tried to squeeze in through the door when we let him in. It was quite a chore pushing them off as they tried to take over his family perks.

Missy was too busy with her own litter to demand a lot of attention from us. She ate her inside meals hurriedly, and often settled for a quicker meal at the feeder with her brood. They were getting to be quite spunky with definite minds of their own.

Of all the cat family, Calico was the saddest case. Missy and Pooh were getting old, but they were still cocky and assertive. Calico had inherited her mother's cataracts, but apparently did not have the will to overcome her handicap. She allowed the other cats to push her around and keep her from the feeder and water dish. Often she had to sneak into a corner under the upper porch to escape her tormentors. Pooh also favored that particular area for his quiet moments, and he would usually grumble at her before accepting her company. Missy detested Calico and the younger cat was careful to keep a wary distance between them. Tiger, however, could frighten Missy even though he was much smaller. He, alone, kept her worried by his presence. It appeared that size had nothing to do with the pecking order!

With the decline of Missy and Pooh, the family of cats were jockeying for the dominant positions the old timers had held for so many years. A family feud was developing. The February litter was fighting for top rank despite the fact that Black and White Daddy and Big Red were more mature. These older males showed no signs of natural leadership. Tiger seemed to be marching towards the job of top cat with Lilipooh pressing for the position of matriarch. Missy, with Pooh backing her up, was fighting this changing of the guard.

Our week with Becky and Arlene passed quickly and it was time to see them off on Chalks Airline. The next day offered us the calm we needed for our smaller plane, so it was time for us, also, to leave the island. We had given two litters of kittens a good start in life and we left pleased that we had played a part in their early development.

Chapter 22

As we pulled up to Echo House in Clyde Flowers' pick-up truck on November 1, 1988, we spotted one of the babies from Lilipooh's litter running across the yard. It was as large as the mother had been last summer. We hoped its twin would show up. They would have to be together in order to know both still existed, since they were identical clones of Pooh and lacked the touches of white fur that made their mother such a fetching female.

Before we had finished unloading supplies our old friend Pooh made an appearance. We had barely finished greeting and accepting him into the house when Missy gave us a vocal "hello". She came in and joined Pooh, in an intertwined dance of affection. When Pooh tired of her persistent attention, flopped on the floor next to the food dishes. Missy continued to nuzzle him, butting heads and licking him until he could take no more. Suddenly he rose to his feet, stretching until he loomed over her looking twice her size. She quickly cowered beneath his male dominance. Pooh relaxed and retreated to the corner of the kitchen, indicating he wanted peace and quiet while he waited for his food to be served.

Since I had to get the chicken thawed in the microwave and then cut it up into bite size pieces, the job dragged out. Unable to contain herself, Missy began again annoying Pooh with more of her head butting. Pooh lashed out at her with his claws extended and she bristled her fur and hissed in a shrewish voice. At this point I broke up the domestic altercation by giving them their bowls of food. Tranquility returned as they rushed to gobble the food. After the usual confusion as to who got which bowl, they finally made their selections and crouched to enjoy their delicacies. After they finished they strolled into the living room and settled down on the rug like two domesticated cats.

At the rear sliding doors, Lilipooh and a strange new black and white cat were staring in with hungry eyes that begged for food. Norm opened a fresh bag of dried food and filled the feeder. As soon as he reentered the house, they headed for the feeder and ate with the frenzy of starvation. When they finished, I put a bowl of water outside and they were as grateful as they had been for the food. This new friend, or more likely mate, of Lilipooh's appeared to be an offspring of Black and White Daddy. His fur was thick and

Chapter 22

soft, but it failed to lie close to his body, giving him a frizzled appearance, thus he was named Fuzzy.

While Missy and Pooh enjoyed their morning inside with us, Lilipooh and Fuzzy hung around outside near the door. We finally forced Missy and Pooh outside after lunch, much to their displeasure.

At the crack of dawn the next morning we woke up to find four cats peering at us through the glass bedroom doors. As soon as they saw us get out of bed, they headed down to the lower porch to await breakfast. We fooled them by dressing and then sneaking down the back stairs to the garage. We took out our bikes and pedaled away for our morning ride. When we returned, our cat friends were still patiently waiting for us, showing great restraint over our unnecessary delay. We let the two older cats inside when we had their food ready. They were so greedy and nasty about sharing that we chased Missy outside and put her dish on the porch. She was so indignant she left the porch and Fuzzy happily settled down to eat her breakfast. Without his mate's distraction, Pooh ate properly and then settled on the love seat for a morning nap.

Midmorning Norm tried to hand feed Lilipooh, but she was very wary and refused to come near his hand, forcing him to drop the treats on the floor

Friday morning we were returning from Tower House in our golf cart when we spotted Pooh trotting towards us. The cart startled him and he jumped off the side of the road. Ever since the road had been paved two years ago, the island animals, chickens, turkeys, peacocks and cats have considered it their special domain. They wait until the last possible moment to jump out of the way of vehicles. As we passed an indignant looking Pooh, I yelled at him, "It's lunch time, come home!"

He disappeared into the thicket and when we pulled up to the garage he was already at the front door waiting to get inside. Missy turned up moments later.

When the Maier's came for dinner Sunday night there was lots of talk about our cats and their cats. With more than fifty cats to feed, Doc Maier told us he was going to work harder than ever to get a veterinarian and his assistant, who were friends of his, to come to the island and neuter a lot of the cats. It wouldn't be an easy job to round up so many wild animals, however he believed they could do it. When Missy and Pooh came inside to eat, Carl Maier observed her eye condition and told us some of his cats had the same problem. Because of the closed community of cats on the island, many of them exhibited the same physical ailments.

Pooh, Missy and Fuzzy continued to be a threesome; Fuzzy being a very young adult always stayed in the background, but never too far away from his protectors. He was quite definitely not in partnership with Lilipooh, she showed as much dislike for him as Missy showed for her. On Sunday, November 6, Lilipooh failed to show up at the house. Four days later she was still missing and it was apparent that Missy had driven her away. It was on the morning of November 9 that we noticed Missy was in the wood pile where Lilipooh had raised her kittens last summer. Suddenly, at her call, two doddering kittens popped out of the

Chapter 22

wood pile and stood staring at us. As we watched, Fuzzy strolled into the domestic scene and started licking and grooming the little ones. Missy departed, leaving him in full charge. One kitten was calico, the other black and white like Missy. We now understood why Fuzzy and Missy wanted Lilipooh out of the way!

A lifetime affection still remained between Missy and Pooh, even though their instincts told them that too many generations of kittens from one union was bad for the cat race. For the past couple of years they had chosen other partners for mating without losing the deep affection they felt for each other. Obviously they felt a closeness to each other's litters of babies. They also accepted each other's part time partners as part of their enlarged family. Once the kittens were weaned, however, they went to great lengths to drive out the part time sexual partners so they could resume their usual twosome. During the non-mating season only Pooh and Missy, and the children they happened to favor at the time, continued to live in their territory. Missy, being considerably younger, and stronger than Pooh determined and controlled who stayed with them. We were sure at this point that Lilipooh had been given her walking papers by her mother and wouldn't be coming back!

Fuzzy was so young and new at the fathering game that he still wanted Missy to treat him like one of the children. When she nursed the kittens he often sought a spare teat and nursed with them. With only two kittens, she had milk to spare and seemed to enjoy the attention from Fuzzy.

Friday morning I was working in the kitchen when I heard the piercing cry of one of the kittens. Missy, Pooh and Fuzzy were stretched out on the porch, ignoring the cries, so I figured nothing was wrong. Fifteen minutes later, however, with the kitten still wailing, I went outside to investigate. The cries seemed to be coming from the trees behind the porch. I followed the sounds and found the calico kitten clinging to a branch about six feet off the ground. Apparently the three older cats were waiting for the youngster to get itself back to the ground. I couldn't ignore its pleading cries and lifted the tiny blue eyed creature from the limb and carried it back to the wood pile. It dove under the lumber and never reappeared that day. By Saturday morning it had overcome its terror and was upstairs on the porch as curious as ever. The second kitten remained in the woodpile still unable to crawl beyond the nest!

Chapter 23

Sunday morning was calm and beautiful. Weather reports indicated high winds and showers arriving Monday, so we quickly closed up the house and headed for our airplane and home in Boca Raton. When we left we had every good intention of returning in just a few weeks. Consequently we left piles of dirty laundry along with fresh foods in the refrigerator that we figured would last until our next visit.

We came home to many unexpected personal family problems that entangled our lives for the next five months and kept us from Cat Cay. On January 13, 1989 we received a letter from the Maier's indicating they had succeeded in getting the veterinarian and his assistant to come to the island for four days. During that short stay they caught and spayed or neutered thirty-two of the cats living at the Maiers' house. They also took blood samples from two sick cats and discovered that they had feline leukemia. One of the sick ones had to be put to sleep. Since they only dealt with the younger cats, they regretted afterwards that they didn't get blood samples from the cats four years and older. The older cats appear to be much healthier and immune from defects. The Maier's said the woman assistant was experienced in handling wild cats and did a remarkable job of catching, calming and handling the creatures. In those few days they performed a wonderful voluntary service that was much needed on the island. Since the Maier's, like us, are quiet people who stay out of the social life of the island's club membership, others on the island did not know what had taken place to humanely stop the overpopulating of the cats. Unfortunately some of the island people were instigating other, less humane, ways of dealing with the problem.

In February we received reports from friends on the island that one of our long time club members was offering Bahamians $10.00 for every dead cat they delivered to him. While trying to verify the truth of this matter, another member insisted we had heard incorrectly. The $10.00 reward was for dead rats, not dead cats! One story claimed approximately 100 cats were rounded up through the use of "Have a heart" type traps and by Bahamian employees who caught them by hand. These cats were supposed to have been taken by boat to uninhabited South Cat Cay island and set free. One individual, however, doubting the story, went to the other island and found no evidence of any cats, dead or alive.

Chapter 23

It was generally assumed that the animals had been taken to sea and drowned.

With each passing month we were away from Cat Cay I became more worried about our family of cats and their fate. When we finally returned to the island on April 7, 1989, it had been exactly 5 months since our last visit.

Chapter 24

As we approached Cat Cay from the air, we were startled to see the entire north end of the island had been stripped of all growth! The lovely natural forest of trees, except for a few straggly palms that had grown up in recent years, was gone. The narrow end of the island looked tiny and vulnerable in its naked condition. We learned later from Clyde Flowers, Bahamian Manager of the island, that one of the Cuban American club members had bought the area and intended to re-landscape it as he had already done with other property he owned. The man seemed to have an insatiable desire to turn the natural beauty of the little island into a formal manicured scene. For years we had watched him destroy virtually every fiber of natural growth that held the island together, to be replaced with exotic plants that required constant watering and fertilizing. Over the years we watched the shoreline of his property crumble into the ocean because of his removal of the native growth stitching it together. Although the natural seashore growth is protected by Bahamian law, the government of the tiny island nation is too small to enforce most of their ecological regulations. Non citizens have been free to come into the country and try to convert it into the same kind of polished disaster created in Florida! Since the non-native landscaping required constant watering, on an island that receives very little rain during the year, wells have been sunk into the island's rocky foundation to supply brackish water to feed it. Although native growth has adapted to drought conditions over the years, and survives the sometimes month-long-periods without rain, the imported plantings suffer. The large stripped areas look like abandoned battlefields during the winter dry season. Where imported bushes and trees have been planted, it is a major job replacing those that quickly die off.

Although most island visitors have applauded this new landscaping, which, while it flourishes, makes the place look like a stateside golf course, Norm and I have been apprehensive. We withheld our concerns except to a few close friends. We have lived through some pretty severe hurricanes in the past and respect what their fury can do to man's work. The new trees and shrubs will be more vulnerable to such storms than the natural growth that survived over the centuries. More and more shore erosion is already occurring and the openness of the formally

Chapter 24

landscaped areas will lead to precious soil being washed away by heavy rains and high winds. At the same time, buildings on the island will lose the protection once afforded by the rugged natural growth surrounding them.

This desire to manicure all the available land is also wiping out the world of the island cats. They have thrived for several hundred years because of the thick wild growth and the abundant food chain it nurtured. The impenetrable thickets have protected their families, giving them cover in which to hunt and hide. All that is rapidly disappearing. Soon the entire island will be covered with homes and neat, grassy formal lawns, just like Florida. The only factor that might slow this headlong rush to create another Miami is the lack of fresh water and the high cost of desalinization.

In all the years we have stayed at Cat Cay, we have depended upon the natural shade of the trees around our houses and the gentle whirl of ceiling fans, open doors and windows to keep us cool and comfortable. Most of our new neighbors, living on their cleared lots, bake in the sun or huddle behind the sealed doors and windows of their air conditioned houses.

Because the island had been suffering through a prolonged drought that started the previous fall, we found Echo House free of mildew and insect life. At least it made it easier to clean up the place and make it liveable.

It was sheer delight to be back as we opened all the doors and windows and immediately filled the cat feeder. We really had faith in our cat friends, confident they would show up soon!

It was late afternoon when Pooh came by, thin but healthy. I got very emotional when I let the old guy inside and called for Norm to come and see him. Pooh wasn't impressed by my out flowing of love and resisted my attempts to hug him. The first business on his agenda was food! Norm had filleted a large red snapper earlier in the day, saving the scraps. Pooh made short order of these choice morsels, while Norm put the fish head and stripped carcass out on the back porch. By the time Pooh finished his meal and left the house, two of his children had found the other fish parts and were working over them. Pooh, who was as full as a cat could get, lazily sprawled at the edge of the porch and watched the kids strip the remaining meat from the fish.

We had to wait until lunch time the next day before Missy showed up. She ignored the porch feeder and cried to come inside. Although she enjoyed her meal, she was obviously not starving and one serving was sufficient. Like Pooh, she was anxious to eat and leave. It would take a few days before the cats would spend much time at our place. It was quite apparent that other families were taking care of their needs and we were just another stop on their route. If they decided we were offering better fair than the other stops, we would once again become the location of choice. We understood their practical approach. After all we hadn't been around for almost half a year.

By April 9 we were conscious of a new pattern of behavior in our cats. Pooh and Missy were being very careful to arrive for their meals at different times, not once

Chapter 24

did they arrive together. Neither of them showed any interest in hanging around. After eating their meals in a very businesslike manner they quickly disappeared. This routine continued until the morning of April 11, when they arrived together. When they came inside they acted a bit embarrassed with each other as though they hadn't intended to end up together. They quickly ate everything I had to offer and disappeared in different directions when they left. Around noon they both reappeared for lunch and afterwards retreated to the back porch were they lolled around at opposite ends, continuing to ignore each other.

Late in the afternoon a large red cat with white paws and bib joined Missy. She had to be our Lilipooh! During the past five months she had filled out and matured, now rivaling Missy in size and shape. Lilipooh settled down comfortably next to her mother, the two seemed to be back on good terms with each other!

Our old friend Pooh pretty much ignored us for the next two days. He showed up just once on the back porch, making a lot of noise but refusing to come inside. He ate his fill at the feeder. Missy continued to stay away from him, but continued to come inside for her meals.

Although we saw little cat activity around the house, the rapid disappearance of food from the feeder indicated that many cats were taking advantage of it when we weren't around to see them. As a matter of fact, the food was vanishing at an alarming rate!

It was apparent, as we rode or walked along the north end of the island on the old road, that there were far more cats than we normally saw in that territory. Upon nosing around we learned that the Bahamians, who were given the job of disposing of the captured cats, had quietly brought them to the north end of the island and released them rather than slaughter them as ordered. Residents on that end of the island, which has always been more primitive in its growth than the more populated southern portion, have always been friendlier to the creatures than their neighbors to the south. The Bahamians readily admit to loving the long time cat residents of their island and don't want to harm them!

On April 14, Pooh showed up and came inside for lunch. After I prepared a special treat and placed it on the floor for him, he flipped his tail at me in disdain and went back outside to eat at the feeder!

The next morning Pooh made a very noisy arrival. When he got our attention he gave us a cat lecture in very angry terms, all the while refusing our invitations to come inside. He squirted his scent all around the porch, on posts and furniture, as we yelled at him to no avail. When he was satisfied with the intensity of the nasty odor, he flipped his tail at us and stalked down the porch stairs, all the while screaming at us in an angry staccato. We decided he had only called on us and eaten inside for a few days to prove he still had house privileges. Now he was showing us he didn't need our friendship any more! He had other places where he could visit and get a good meal. We were being punished for staying away for such a long time!

After lunch I walked out the back door and startled Calico at the feeder. She ran down the stairs, but stopped and

Chapter 24

stared when I talked to her. Like Lilipooh, she had grown much larger than her parents' generation. With so many more people living on the island, the younger generation of cats was eating better and growing almost as large as mainland cats.

Missy showed up for an early lunch the morning of April 16. Norm served her a bowl of chicken bits and while she was eating sneaked up behind her and touched her back. She sprang into the air, twisting to face him with her sharp claws extended. She put on a terrifying performance of snarling and hissing, but Norm didn't back off. Instead, he snarled back at her, yelling, "Cut it out Missy, I'm your friend and give you treats!" Missy immediately calmed down, staring intently at him. Finally she quietly returned to the dish and finished eating

I got out some soft cat food, put it in a dish and took it out on the porch. Not a cat was in sight, but as I went back inside I could see several of them coming out of their hiding places under the upper porch. They were Calico, Lilipooh and a strange new calico female. Moments later Pooh arrived and came inside. Norm prepared a meal for him, but before he could put it on the floor Pooh had dashed back outside. He got into an angry hissing match with Calico who stood her ground firmly until he gave up, strolling away without a thought for the meal waiting inside for him.

The next day Pooh and the new calico female showed up together. He was very attentive to her needs and guarded the area while she ate at the feeder. We noticed her teats were heavy with milk. Missy kept in the background, showing no animosity towards the younger female, but when Pooh walked too close to her she snarled and chased him back to his new girl friend. Even though, for the time, they were no longer mates, they made it clear they were going to maintain their rights to the territory. For the past three years instinct had been forcing them apart for the good of their offspring. Finally they seemed to have severed their emotional bonds with each other. Not withstanding the changed relationship, they continued to have great respect for each other and intended to stay close together. They had both come to fairly good terms with the last litter they had together and only occasionally had arguments with Lilipooh and Calico who were now permanent fixtures in the territory. We did not see the other cats like Black and White Daddy, Junior nor the litters of kittens born last summer, anywhere in the area . We feared that some of them had succumbed to the island cat roundup.

Early the next morning we were awakened by meowing and scratching noises. We suspected that Pooh and Calico had a family hidden away from sight. Pooh apparently believed that we had accepted his new mate and he confidently brought her to the door at breakfast time. We let him inside, but kept her out in deference to Missy. We put an extra dish of chicken bits on the porch which Pooh's new mate attacked with relish. When their meals were finished they strolled off together, lovingly rubbing each other along the way. It seemed strange to see Pooh emotionally involved with someone other than Missy. In the past he had mated with other females but had never shown any real affection for

Chapter 24

them. Even long after Missy had taken other partners like Black and White Daddy and Fuzzy, Pooh still claimed her as his mate. Now the bond appeared to be finally broken and the new calico female was the apple of his eye. We found it rather amazing that such a young attractive female would chase such an elderly partner! He certainly was not the macho looking, and acting, cat he once was!

Before we left the island we made every possible effort to find the new offspring of Pooh and the new calico. Although we could hear their squeals somewhere near our bedroom, we never solved the mystery of their location. Hopefully we will come back in July and learn how Pooh and Missy are coping with their separation.

Chapter 25

Pooh was the first to visit us after we arrived at Echo House on June 30, 1989. The weather had turned stormy by noon and he was drenched to the skin, emphasizing his scrawniness. He was skittish and anxious to bolt down his meal and leave. I observed bloody scars all over his head as he ate the meal. The old warrior was still surviving, but he was not a pretty sight!

A short while later Missy, a handsome young red male, and their black and white kitten arrived at the back door. Missy accepted our invitation to come in and eat while her mate and the kitten stared at us through the screen door. They were obviously accustomed to close contact with humans because they stood their ground when I put a bowl of cat food on the porch for them.

Each day of our stay more cats showed up. Pooh had two adolescent children who showed great affection for him, they were both handsome well formed cats. One was a calico and the other a pale red tiger with white chest and paws. They showed great togetherness, tenderly bumping heads with each other and curling up for naps together snuggled close on the chaise lounge. We knew the two youngsters were males because they tried to mount the black and white female every time she got out of Missy's jurisdiction. The poor thing had a hard time fighting off their eager attentions, she wanted no part of them, being too young to mate.

The weather continued to be stormy and cool during our visit and the cats spent most of their time on the porches. Norm enjoyed feeding them by hand as they all seemed semi-tame and obviously spent a lot of time with the workmen next door. They lived sumptuously, eating all the food that was offered at both homes. We knew there were additional cats who came up to the porch feeder at night that we didn't see during the day.

Even though Missy and Pooh were selecting different mates they were being drawn back together. At times they acted like young lovers rediscovering each other after a spat. They smooched in an outrageous and uninhibited manner right in front of Missy's new mate. He accepted their actions with dignity and showed no animosity. When the two old cats came inside their affection was a dance of love. They intertwined with each other as they delighted in their renewed relationship. They even stretched out together and slept for long periods on the hearth rug while we worked at our

Chapter 25

household tasks. The rains poured and the winds blew, but inside our home tranquility reigned between us and our favorite cats!

When the weather turned better and we had to return to the mainland, it was difficult to say goodbye to our two house cats!

Chapter 26

We next visited our island on Thursday August 17, 1989. The weather was extremely hot and seas were calm. When we arrived at Echo House, a small black and white clone of Missy was sitting guard on the front porch. It fled as soon as we approached the house. Once inside our first duty was to fill bowls with dried food and water and place them on the back porch. All day we watched a sad array of scrawny cats come to the bowls for a nourishing meal. Pooh was a late arrival, looking healthy despite his leanness. He demanded his right to join us inside for his meal. It took several helpings of food to fill him, but once he was satisfied he was in an excellent frame of mind. He enjoyed being tickled and talked to and responded by rubbing against my legs.

After a short visit with us, Pooh was anxious to leave and I let him out. A large red tiger with white bib and paws was standing by one of the empty food dishes with a look of despair. Feeling sorry for him I refilled the dish. Pooh was watching what I did and the minute I set the dish down he stepped forward and growled at the tiger. He was determined to stop the other cat from eating, but I intervened. Scolding him for his selfishness, I pushed him away so the other cat could eat. Pooh didn't resist my actions but retreated to a corner where he could pout and observe the other cat. When the newcomer had his fill and left the food dish, a scrawny black and white kitten wobbled out of its hiding place and headed for the food. It was painfully thin and had great difficulty walking. The dried cat food was a new experience and the poor creature choked and coughed as it tried to swallow the harsh meal. After a largely unsuccessful effort it gave up and drank some water to clear its throat. Exhausted from the activity it just flopped on the floor and went to sleep. Several times during the afternoon it roused itself and ate and drank small amounts of food and water. We were gratified to see it still had the desire to live. The next day I filled a small dish with food and put in near this kitten we now called "Tiny". She realized it was for her and accepted it with renewed confidence. We kept an eye out for the other cats and discouraged any of them from going near that dish. They quickly learned that Tiny owned that dish and it was off limits to them. After two days of nourishment we could see improvement in Tiny's health and became hopeful that she would survive.

It took a while to sort out our new collection of cat friends. There were two red tigers with white bibs and paws,

Chapter 26

one the size of Pooh and one considerably smaller. There were two black and white cats, one fully grown and the other the sickly baby. There was also one grey tiger that hung close to Pooh, the two of them spending their days sleeping together on the upper porch. The big red and the two black and whites seemed to be a family unit. They took their naps together and frequently indulged in affectionate nose rubbing. Now that there apparently was plenty of food they also took their meals together. Daddy usually finished first and then enjoyed sniffing the females while they continued to eat.

Saturday morning Pooh came in for breakfast and stayed with us all day. He was in a mellow mood and demanded a lot of loving attention. I noted that it was 9:15 A.M. when he jumped up on the love seat to sleep. He stretched out full length and slept soundly until noon, ignoring our activities around him.

Several times during the morning I glanced out and saw Tiny making an effort to eat. She slept near her dish, and when awake found just standing up to eat was all the activity she could handle. Even though her food intake was increasing she still had a problem with hiccups, her frail body heaving for as long as a half hour after eating. Fortunately she instinctively limited her intake and managed to survive without throwing up. Occasionally she tried to join the other cats at their food dish, but they made it clear they resented her presence and she would wobble back to her bowl and collapse.

By noon the weather had turned to rain and all the cats were enjoying the shelter of the porches. Norm tried to get their attention with some hand held treats, Little Red was the only one aggressive enough to accept the challenge. In his eagerness, he snapped the food and Norm's fingers at the same time, so that game ended quickly, and the treats were placed on the floor. Big Red paced at a distance while he eyed Little Red grabbing all the goodies. Tiger stayed on the upper stairs and watched with indifference. All the while Pooh continued with his afternoon nap on the love seat. Norm and I decided to go to the work shop to pursue some shell projects, leaving the cats to lounge and sleep away the rainy cool afternoon.

Sunday morning our missing Missy showed up with Pooh at our bedroom door. We were delighted to see her looking healthy and showing her old affection for Pooh. We had no idea why she waited so long to show up. The two of them enjoyed a breakfast of turkey leftovers while I filled the food dishes on the porch. All the cats were now assembled and ate according to their pecking order. Tiny was looking much stronger and even toddled over to the regular eating dish. She was allowed to feed at the community dish after all the others were finished and she seemed to thoroughly enjoy the new privilege.

Mid morning Missy showed up with a second kitten, who's condition was not much better than Tiny's. Apparently she had been keeping this one hidden below the house. It was another red tiger with white bib and feet. The new baby and

Chapter 26

Tiny approached the food dish to eat, causing Big Red, Medium Red and the grey tiger to move in and harass the kids. Missy sprang up, raising her hackles, and hissed at them. They immediately backed off, then slowly crept away while Missy continued to snarl and scold. In all the years we had known Missy we had never seen another cat attempt to attack her or refuse to obey her orders to back off. She was truly a Margaret Thatcher of the cat world!

When Rosa arrived with her broom to sweep the walks clean, I went down for a visit. She said the day before we arrived she came to the house and found Pooh sitting on the front porch looking very wise. She told him, "Your people aren't here, so why are you hanging around?" He didn't budge and just blinked at her as though to say, "I know something you don't!"

She noted how thin he was and told me she was tempted to go home and get some cat food for him. Since the cats never hang around the house when we are gone, she felt he somehow knew we were due to arrive.

Monday morning Pooh greeted us at the bedroom door when we woke up. He and the black and white kitten were our only guests until dinner. Norm had some lobster scraps to give the cats for lunch. Tiny got her share on the porch and showed how wise she was becoming by quickly devouring them before someone else showed up!

At dinner time Missy showed up with still another scrawny red tiger kitten. This one was full of spunk and fought for its right to eat with the others. Missy made sure that it got its fair share.

After finishing our supper I opened up the sticky ice cream carton with its melting remnants of vanilla ice cream, and put it on the porch. Two of the kittens had a delightful time licking it clean. They walked all over the sticky surface getting as messy as human children. The older cats looked on in disgust, finally leaving one by one. The kittens spent the evening on the porch cleaning and grooming their gummy fur. It was a tough job, but they looked presentable again by the time the adults reappeared.

Once again, on Tuesday morning, Pooh was waiting to wake us up. We let him in, got dressed and went downstairs where Missy was anxiously waiting to get inside. I was completely out of food scraps and had to give the cats prepared cat food. They were highly indignant at this turn of events, Pooh angrily batted my legs while Missy hissed in displeasure. I was so upset I walked out and left them. Later when I quietly returned they were calmly eating the dried cat food. The three kittens on the porch were also in a cantankerous mood. The red ones invaded Tiny's dish and she was forced to eat from the regular bowl. When she did that they rushed over to push her away. I chased the reds off the porch and didn't let them return until Tiny had finished eating.

The next day we knew we had to return home while the weather remained calm. Sadly, we didn't think Tiny would survive once we were gone.

Chapter 27

Our cat family was sprawled across the back porch when we arrived October 2, 1989. It was obvious they were getting plenty of food and water. We didn't learn until the next morning, when Rosa arrived on her bicycle with a jug of water and a bag of cat food, that she was their benefactor. We were delighted and gave her the money she needed to purchase a fresh supply of food. She told us she ordered a shipment of cat food from Nassau once a month. It arrived by boat with other supplies for the island. When she filled the dishes on the porch the cats gathered around her and some of them even let her pet them. They all jabbered at her at once as she poured the food.

Wonder of wonders, her favorite was Tiny, now a shy but beautiful female adolescent. She still demanded her own food dish in an isolated corner of the porch. She had become a loner, never associating with her siblings, remembering well her early weeks when they blocked her out. Her only show of affection was towards her mother Missy. She constantly shadowed Missy's movements and the older cat accepted the close relationship.

Missy and Pooh were pleased to have us back and they moved inside each day to become house cats. It was a time of year when their mating instincts were dormant and they were calm in their personal relationship, Pooh spending the afternoons sleeping on the love seat while Missy sprawled on the living room rug.

The red tiger cats with white bibs were a constant threesome on the porch. Two of them we identified as from Lillipooh and her mate, the third was smaller and had to be from the same litter as Tiny.

The two males adored Lillipooh and always waited until she finished eating before they ate. The grey and black tiger sat and watched with a worried look, since he didn't get a meal if they ate all the food. He sometimes growled and grumbled if they were eating too much, but never asserted himself physically.

Thursday morning I was working in the ground floor workshop. I could hear Missy scolding outside. I peeked out the window and spotted her in the side yard with a kitten. Since she had not been pregnant last August, this was a mystery kitten. It's physical appearance was unusual, all white except for a few large blotches of red and black fur. I estimated it was about four weeks old. When I went outside to get a better look, it scampered into the thicket and disappeared never to be seen again. It was terribly thin and I wondered why it wasn't getting more nourishment from its mother.

Each time we have visited the island since our purchase of Echo House nine years ago, we have always found Missy and Pooh in charge. In recent years as Pooh's strength diminished, Missy had become the dominant figure. It is she alone, who determines who shares the territory with her and her mate Pooh. The males seem to obey her edicts without question, for we have never seen her involved physically in a dispute with any of them. She has always kept herself surrounded with healthy young males who honored her superior ranking. Occasionally she accepted the friendship of another female of lesser standing, like her daughter Tiny. We have concluded that the cat population changes from time to time when certain males and females decide to break away from Missy's dominance and strike out on their own in some other territory. Since Missy must be 7 or 8 years old and suffers from very poor eyesight, we wonder how much longer she can control her little world. Certainly Pooh's well being is dependent upon her strength. Every time he gets into a fight he comes out with serious injuries. Knowing his limitations he has been avoiding controversy and tries to exist without triggering anger in the younger cats. He's very careful not to approach the food or water dishes on the porch when the other cats are hungry or thirsty. Inside the house we have to give him meals while Missy is outside, since even she will push him aside and take his share.

We suspect that Lillipooh and her mate will be the successors to the monarchy when Missy gives up. Lillipooh has lasted longer than any other female and she is a very dominant personality. Missy tolerates her because I think she realizes she is not strong enough to drive the younger female away. When all the cat family is on the porch, however, Missy still eats first and Lillipooh is second. All the males instinctively know the females deserve the best diet so they can produce healthy offspring.

A cat community maintains a rigid pecking order and the size of the group depends upon the availability of food. The food Rosa provides is enough for 7 to 8 adult cats and that is exactly the size of Missy's clan. Occasionally we hear a confrontation in the night and we know an outsider is trying to join the group. On those occasions the entire community will unite to drive out the intruder cat. On the other hand, when a member leaves by choice, Missy allows their place to be filled by a newcomer.

Our visit with the cats was cut short by a prediction of bad weather. As so often happens we had to pack up fast and leave before the winds and ocean kicked up.

Chapter 28

We arrived on the island the morning of February 7, 1990. The moment we opened the door to Echo House we knew our refrigerator had stopped running. The sickening odor of spoiled food permeated the atmosphere. Missy and Pooh were crying at the back door to come in, but we had to ignore them in the face of the major emergency that we had encountered. I opened the refrigerator door and almost fainted from the foul odor and the sight of swarming maggots. Norm closed the door and told me that we'd have to find Clyde and get the refrigerator hauled out of the house. It was afternoon before Clyde got a truck and crew to take away the offensive appliance and bring a substitute we could use during our visit. It was fortunate we had brought enough fresh food with us to take care of our needs along with the canned stuff already on the kitchen shelves.

Happily for our cat friends, we even had some frozen chicken scraps with us we could thaw for their meal. When we finally invited them inside to eat I noted that Pooh had deep scratches all over his head and back. His fur was thinning out making his battle wounds all the more visible. Since Missy was obviously pregnant, Pooh must have had to fight for the right to father yet another batch of kittens. His continued virility amazed us.

On the porch to greet us at dinner time were two of the kittens from last summer, the calico and Black and White. Lillipooh and her red tiger mate also showed up. A second pair of red tigers with white bibs and feet arrived moments later and confused us because they looked so much like Lillipooh and her mate. The female of this new pair was a flirt, she enjoyed letting the males, including Pooh, smell her private areas. This behavior upset her mate and he became very vocal about it. His distress was particularly apparent when Pooh showed special attention to his female. The two males fussed at each other each time this happened. Finally, after several days of this heavy talk, the younger cat blew his top and attacked Pooh. Cat fur was flying all over the porch when I intervened by grabbing Pooh in my arms and taking him into the house. He was grateful for the rescue and happy to stretch out on the living room rug for the rest of the evening.

At night when the house was lighted and the porch dark, our cats enjoyed people watching. They all took turns

Chapter 28

standing near the screen doors and staring intently as we moved about inside.

On the whole, our cat family got along with each other. When one of them got out of line, however, by not following the proper pecking order, the others expressed concern. Calico and Black and White, being the youngsters of the group, shared end of the line eating rights. Being young and frisky they liked to test their elders by sneaking in early for their meals. Rosa filled a large cake pan with cat food every other day. This food had to take care of the cats until she returned.

By the middle of the second day the supply was usually getting low and pecking order became very important. The younger cats ended up hungry unless they could beat the system. If we had extra scraps we could share, we added these to the remains of the dried food. This helped to keep peace until the pan was filled the next day, easing the internecine warfare.

During this visit Norm and I began to discuss the idea that we should give up Echo House. Our family no longer wanted to spend their vacations there and transportation to the island was becoming difficult since Chalks Airline stopped making regular flights. Without Chalks big seaplanes we no longer had a way to get friends to the island unless we chartered a plane to bring them, which in most cases was not practical.

Tower House was much smaller and easier to maintain, offering everything that Norm and I needed during our infrequent visits to the island. It was our love for the cats and

Rosa's willingness to feed and look after them that caused us to hesitate over selling Echo House. After this visit to the island, we transferred our base of operations to Tower House and only returned to Echo House to visit our cat family.

While we were staying at Tower House in July, 1990, our friends the Maier's were also spending some time at their home. They were eager to tell us how they had just about solved the problem of the cat overpopulation on Cat Cay. They had invited their veterinarian friends back for two more visits. Between the two couples, they captured, one at a time, virtually every cat on the island. They anesthetized each cat, neutered it and kept it captive in the bottom of the Maiers' empty swimming pool until it recovered. The only cats they didn't try to catch were our small family at Echo House. They wanted us to know what they were doing before they touched our friends. We said it was fine to neuter all but Missy and Pooh, whom we considered too old to survive surgery. Dr Maier told us everyone on the island was happy with this solution. Folks now felt comfortable feeding and looking out for the cats knowing they weren't helping to increase the population. The cats stopped their night-time wailing and the spraying of male odor all over the island. Fighting between courting males had come to an end.

Of course, they couldn't get to all the cats, there would always be a few like Missy and Pooh who escaped the surgeon's knife. These would continue the island's cat population at a reduced rate, it would be many years before Cat Cay would once more face an explosion of the cat population.

Chapter 28

We eventually sold Echo House in early 1991. By then Rosa had retired and returned to Nassau. Our cat family quickly scattered to other homes where handouts were available. We still run across Missy and Pooh when we visit their domain on the north end of the island. Both are natural survivors and doing fine. We have to believe Pooh is the oldest cat on Cat Cay. There will never be another cat who can take his place.

He is, and always will be, Top Cat on Cat Cay!

* * * * *

Post Script — Norman E. Wymbs

Harriet wound up the last chapter feeling she had completed her saga of the cats of Cat Cay. As is so often true in life, fate was ready to take a hand and write another chapter. Since Harriet did not participate in some of the events to follow, she asked me to append this addition to her story.

During the summer of 1992 we spent a delightful three weeks at Tower House, fishing, diving and occasionally checking our old cat friends on the north end of the Island. Since we depended upon our Lake-Amphibian to fly back and forth, we, as always, kept a close check on the weather. During the summer we were almost guaranteed clear weather and calm seas for our seaplane. We never forgot, however, that this beautiful summer weather also spawned rainy and windy tropical storms, so were always prepared to leave on short notice.

That August the tropics were normally active and by the 18th the Weather Service was tracking a depression in the eastern Atlantic. We decided to fly home the next day after securing our boat and Tower House. The tropical storm now had a name, "Andrew", but was so far away and small it appeared to pose no threat other than rising seas which made amphibious aircraft uncomfortable. Having completed our normal allotment of three weeks on the Island, on August 19 we flew back to Florida. By now the National Hurricane Center in Coral Gables, Florida was issuing regular reports on "Andrew" and forecasting imminent hurricane status.

The storm was growing in strength but it remained quite limited in the area it covered. There was little concern in south Florida since the storm seemed to be missing all the eastern Caribbean islands and the prime time TV programs lacked their usual exciting pictures of wind blown debris and crashing surf.

Following Hurricane Andrew's progress we were relieved to see it by-passing the heavily populated eastern Bahamas, but began to feel some apprehension about what path it would follow through the western islands containing Cat Cay. As it whirled westward, our concern in that area was lessened when it became obvious that Andrew would strike south Florida.

Harriet and I closed up our Boca Raton home with heavy storm shutters and prepared to move inland to stay at our son's home on higher ground to the west. During the afternoon of August 24, 1992, we huddled with Paul, Heidi and granddaughter Heather around the television as Andrew's journey was documented.

We knew the storm was passing near Cat Cay but were still not too concerned since it was still small in area and our island was such a tiny target in the vast ocean. With the actual point of impact of the storm on south Florida still in doubt, our concern was for the family homes in Boca Raton.

That night, as Andrew came ashore south of Miami, over 70 miles away from us in Boca Raton, Miami's TV stations made it clear that this was one of the most devastating storms to ever strike Florida. One TV station went off the air as its transmitting tower blew down. One station lost its studios and the news and weather commentators were broadcasting from a cramped equipment room at their transmitter. Even the Miami Weather Radar and their forecasting headquarters in Coral Gables were knocked out.

We didn't need TV and radio to tell us how bad it was down there, since 70 miles from the storm's center we were losing trees and building parts as the storm messed up our neighborhood!

The next morning we listened to radio reports on the virtual destruction of the City of Homestead, south of Miami. Returning to our own home, dragging tree limbs aside so we could get in, we spent the morning opening storm shutters on a bright clear day. As things were getting back to normal, our phone rang. The call was from Clyde Flowers, via radiotelephone from Cat Cay! Although virtually indecipherable through the static, I could recognize Clyde's excited voice, "-------Major damage---------disaster-------Cat Cay gone!" The connection broke off with no further communication.

Now, deeply concerned over conditions on Cat Cay we tried desperately for news from that small part of the world. With the horrible destruction to south Florida, the news media had not had time to consider what damage Andrew might have done on its way to the U.S. mainland. It wasn't until the next day that we began to get news of the island. The Cat Cay Club office in Fort Lauderdale was back in operation, from there we received the first detailed report on what had happened to our little island.

Andrew had passed directly over Cat Cay, with what we later learned were winds in excess of 200 miles per hour. The Florida office advised that, thankfully, no one on the island had been injured. Property damage, with few exceptions, was almost total. They advised that the seaplane ramp had been cleared and Chalk's Airline was preparing to send in emergency flights. An area in the middle of the small golf course had been cleared and helicopters were already on the island.

I advised Harriet that I would fly our seaplane over the next day to survey the situation and check on Tower House. Since Harriet was not feeling well, our son Paul volunteered to fly with me, no small act of intestinal fortitude on his part since he fared poorly in small airplanes! Early on the morning of August 27, barely two days since the passage of Andrew, Paul and I took off headed for Cat Cay.

The flight across the Atlantic Gulfstream was smooth, with the weather as perfect as you could wish for. Occupied with our own churning thoughts as we purred southeastward, it was impossible for either of us to come to grips with the reported devastation on the island. Coming up on our first checkpoint, the larger western Bahamas' island of Bimini, we were surprised to see it showed no indication of storm damage. Less than ten miles from Cat Cay, Andrew had done little more to Bimini than bring down a lot of palm fronds and coconuts!

Later, we were to learn that the Bahamian Prime Minister, newly elected the month before and deeply concerned over this sudden crisis in his islands, had flown over Bimini by helicopter the morning after Andrew. Radio reports from the ground indicated little damage and everything functioning normally. Since Cat Cay had lost all radio and telephone communication, the officials on Bimini took their silence to indicate there was nothing to report. The Prime Minister's helicopter then turned north to check some other islands, meaning it would be another day before Cat Cay's plight was revealed!

Continuing southeast towards out destination, we passed over the smallest of the usable islands in the western Bahamas, Gun Cay. This quarter mile long piece of rock in the Atlantic was occupied by two small stone and concrete buildings and a 500 ft. tall state of the art radio antenna. Here, for several years the United States and Bahamian Governments had operated a sophisticated tracking and communication system to intercept and thwart drug smugglers bound for Florida. It had been a shining example of inter-government cooperation, sadly now severely hampered as we noted the antenna twisted into a tangled mass of steel draped across the island into the ocean.

Viewing our island as we approached from the north, it became immediately evident that little of its former lush tropical growth remained. Usually, from the air, it appeared as a deep green boomerang shaped landmark nestled in the sparkling blue ocean, with only a few neat rooftops protruding through the cover. Today the green was gone, and stark white sand with scattered dark tree stumps and branches presented a disheartening picture. Flying over at 200 ft. above the ground we found ourselves staring down into the interiors of what had been comfortable homes. That many of houses were totally without roofs was bad enough, even worse were those locations where the buildings had completely disappeared!

Approaching the center of the island we could see that the marina, usually a geometrically neat lineup of boat docks, was now a debris laden bay with no sign of the docks. The harbor breakwater, which had been enlarged during the past two years into a small airport, had reverted again to mostly ocean. Swinging sharply around the south end of the Cay we were relieved to see our Tower House standing like a bright white sentinel on its rocky point. Even the roof appeared unharmed, with its wood shake shingles intact, as we realized our view was enhanced by the lack of leaves and palm fronds usually shading our home. It appeared the old stone and concrete buildings on that end of the island, over 50 years old, had survived remarkably well compared to the near total destruction of the more modern structures on the north end! So much for current building standards!

The ramp near the marina was clear, so we landed on the calm waters and taxied up to park. All of the Club buildings, dining rooms, bars and offices were a shambles. As we climbed out of our plane, amidst the chaos left by Hurricane Andrew, we were greeted by the club staff who had weathered the storm. As soon as the winds subsided they had emerged from their shelter in the basements of some of the older buildings and had been working around the clock ever since clearing narrow paths to outlying parts of the island. Clyde even had a battered cart operating and drove us down to the point where Tower House stood.

Approaching the little peninsula with our house, the Tower stood out in sharp contrast to the scene of destruction at that end of the island. Most of the trees and decorative plantings around the buildings were down, making it difficult, at first glance, to determine the extent of damage to the structures. Only two of the trees on our point were down, helping to give the appearance that Tower House was virtually untouched. We later concluded that our trees, rooted as they were in near solid rock were not as vulnerable as those on the sandier portions of the island. The building structure was intact, however, many of the window panes had blown out and the interior was flooded by the torrential rains of Andrew.

Despite the almost universal damage from the hurricane winds, Andrew had its whimsical side. In our small, dormered "captain's" room, the opposing windows where Harriet and I worked at our island hobbies showed both the power and the gentleness of the storm. The window panes on Harriet's east side had been the first to go, bursting inward under the storm's pressure. The shattered glass crossed the ten feet to my side, some blowing out the west side window, and some, like shrapnel, penetrating the plastered walls to bury themselves in the wooden wall framing. On my bench, under that blown out window, I had left some sea anemone shells (locally called sea biscuits). They were still right where I had left them, still intact although more fragile than egg shells! Andrew had destroyed both windows, ripped pictures and window blinds from their moorings, tumbled and broke furniture, but left those fragile skeletons unmoved on the work bench! In our bedroom, Andrew had shown the same capricious nature, flooding the room with rain water through the broken windows but, unaccountably, leaving our bed and mattress dry, even though under one of those windows!

Paul and I did some basic cleaning up in the Tower and stapled clear plastic over all the broken windows to hold off any more rain damage. Clyde Flowers made copious notes of the work and materials needed to restore our bedraggled home. After doing what we could, we made our slow way on foot back to the marina area and our airplane. At the fork in the road, leading north toward our old Echo House, the way was totally blocked by debris so we couldn't even get through on foot. Some of the property owners had gone to the north end by boat, landing on the beach near what was left of their homes. Their reports indicated even more extensive damage than we had first imagined!

On the way back to our plane we saw one lonely bedraggled cat. One of the Bahamians advised, sadly, that all the cats were lost in the storm. Fortunately his assessment of the resilience of the Cat Cay cats was way off the mark!

On September 9, Harriet and I flew back to Cat Cay for a day to survey progress on the restoration work already under way. Clyde's crew were busily putting Tower House and several others back in shape, so Harriet and I decided to take a run up to Echo House on the now cleared road north. Although the destruction was sobering, there was a bright spot that lifted our spirits.

Along the north road we spotted a number of wary cats, many recognizable as offspring of our old red Pooh and black and white Missy. Although the older cats on the island had not survived, enough of the youngsters had come through Andrew to insure a continuing cat population on Cat Cay!

As we headed back to our plane to return to Florida, we couldn't help but recall how the older cats had prepared their youngsters for just such an emergency. Although there had always been ample food, water and shelter around Echo House we remembered watching Missy patiently teaching her little ones how to catch rats and survive on their own. Even though they were gone, the survival training Pooh and Missy gave their offspring insured the continuation of the long line of Cat Cay cats!

* * * * *

Epilogue

With the passing of Hurricane Andrew and the reconstruction of Cat Cay, I had accepted the fact that I would never again have the opportunity of establishing a close relationship with the Cat Cay cats. Cats had been nearly eradicated on the south end of the island where Tower House is located. Too many people, including the dominant Rockwell family, didn't want any cats around the area.

This situation began to change in 1995. The old, established Club families were thinning out and their properties were being sold to an influx of newer, younger, families. The cats, still propagating on the rest of the island, began to sense the change and gradually moved south again.

At Tower House, we began to see an occasional cat exploring our property. We'd put out food in the evening and it would disappear during the night. On our bike rides around the south end, we often saw containers of dry cat food placed at the edge of the road for the native creatures. When we did spot cats slinking across the yards or golf course, they looked healthy and rotund.

We made a short visit to the island in late February 1996. The weather proved to be the finest the new year had so far offered. It was warm, calm and clear. Even though the water was far too cold for our desire to swim, the bay offered perfect conditions for shell, driftwood, sponge and sea plant collecting. Every day, at low tide, I spent hours in my search for treasures.

The last day of our week's visit, I was concentrating hard since there were so many clusters of shells to explore. I was scrounging the beach in the same area where many years ago an exuberant red cat dashed out of the thicket and established an immediate friendship with me. As I stood there, I observed that the lovely shoreline had all been destroyed. Home owners, wanting easy access to the beach had, over the years, eliminated all this growth, leaving an eroding bluff that would eventually disappear.

As visions of old Pooh flashed before my mind, a whirlwind of black and white fluff came rushing at me from the nearest house. It was a beautiful, half-grown cat, a perfect image of Missie Pooh! I immediately assumed that it had to be a female. As I knelt down, she wrapped her front paws around my legs and looked into my face with the joy and curiosity of youth. After we became acquainted and I had tickled her behind the ears and rubbed her body, we continued a leisurely stroll around the bay. When I had covered my usual distance, we turned around and started to head back. As we approached our original meeting place, my reincarnation of Missie Pooh gave my legs a last embrace before she dashed back to the benefactors who fed her. As I watched her backside galloping away, I was anxious to get back to Norm and tell him of my experience.

I am looking forward to our next visit to the island and to a whole new world of adventure with my beloved cats of Cat Cay!

END

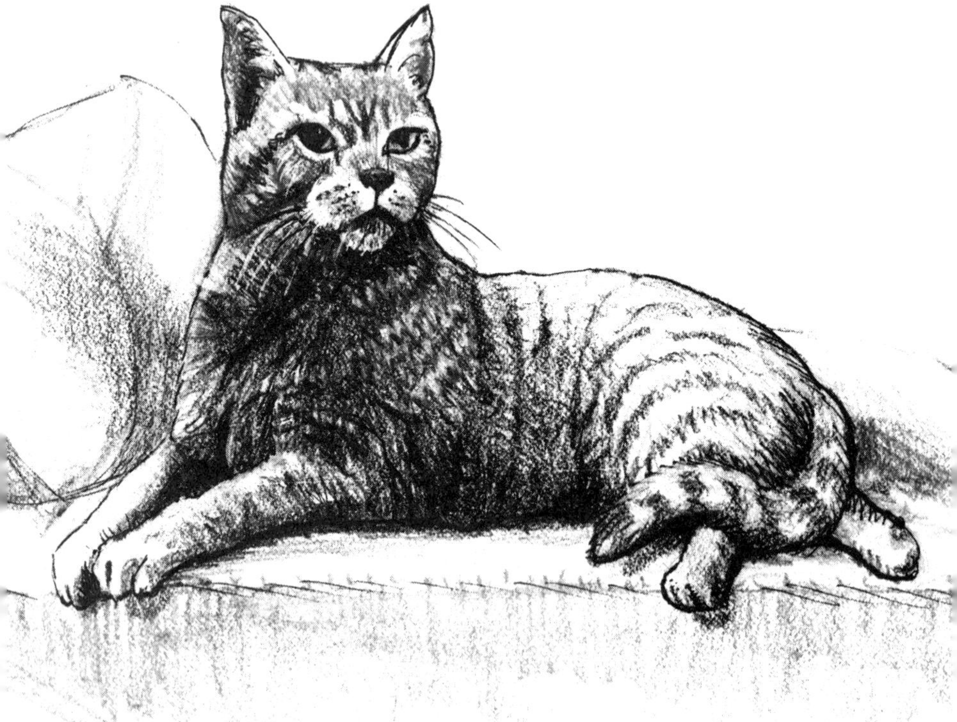